A – Z
OF
PERSONAL FINANCE

NIMI AKINKUGBE

AMVPS

AMVPS

Published by

AMV Publishing Services
P.O. Box 661
Princeton, NJ 08542-0661
Tel: 609-785-5135 Fax: 609-7164770
emails: publisher@amvpublishingservices.com &
customerservice@amvpublishingservices.com
worldwide web: www.amvpublishingservices.com

A-Z Of Personal Finance
Copyright © 2015 Nimi Akinkugbe

For enquiries please contact:
info@moneymatterswithnimi.com
www.moneymatterswithnimi.com
Twitter: @MMWITHNIMI
Instagram: @MMWITHNIMI
Facebook: MoneyMattersWithNimi

Book & Cover Design: AMVPS Origination & Design Division
with assistance on cover design from Dayo Sapoloso

Library of Congress Control Number: 2009912053

Paperback Edition ISBNs: 0-9766941-3-1 (10-Digit)
978-0-9766941-3-7 (13-Digit)
e-Book PDF Edition ISBN: 978-0-9894917-3-0 (13-Digit)
e-Book EPUB Edition ISBN: 978-0-9894917-4-7 (13-Digit)

ENDORSEMENTS

"As Head Private Client Services in Stanbic IBTC, Nimi Akinkugbe was intimately involved in the management of my personal finances. Faithful to the principles brilliantly enunciated in her book, *A-Z Of Personal Finance,* Nimi made me feel comfortable with her inimitable personal touch and professional expertise. I could go to bed, assured that my finances were in capable hands."
> — **Ignatius C. OLISEMEKA**, retired Nigerian Ambassador
> and former Nigerian Foreign Minister

"Opunimi presents personal financial management skills in a practical and engaging way. She will help you manage your money whether you are just starting your first job or are closer to retirement. Opunimi takes you through the important steps involved in securing your future and that of your family."
> —**Ahmed DASUKI,** leading international investor and director of
> several blue chip companies

"There's no magic formula for investing. 'Successful investing requires a well-thought-out plan of action, focus, patience, discipline and a goal.' (Nimi Akinkugbe, *Genevieve* Magazine) The *A-Z Of Personal Finance* is a publication for anyone seeking advice on personal finance, growth and development. To ignore such a valuable manuscript that spells out the A-Z of how you can make your money work for you is a step backwards for any aspiring businessman or woman. Feedback from *Genevieve* readers speak volumes of how Nimi's Money Matters 'A-Z' columns has shaped their financial confidence. I am so excited that we get a book about personal finance that adds tremendous value to its reader. Now, we all have one more reason to take charge of our finances… Personal finance has just become as simple as A to Z."
> — **Betty IRABOR,** Editor-in-Chief, *Genevieve* Magazine

CONTENTS

ACKNOWLEDGEMENTS

I would like to dedicate this text to my beloved parents, Mr & Mrs F. I. Ajumogobia, who engrained in me distinct and invaluable lessons in personal financial management from an early age.

I wish to express my gratitude to all those who encouraged me to write this book; Chief and Mrs. O. I. Akinkugbe, the publications and blogs that provided a platform to present my articles. *Genevieve* Magazine, *234 Next, Business Day* and *Punch* Newspapers, *Forbes Africa* Magazine, BellaNaija.com, LagosMums.com and EdenLifestyle.com formed the basis of the content of this book and for this I am very grateful. The numerous readers of my articles, who took the time to write letters to share their stories, underscored the need for me to compile them into a book for all to read.

I also acknowledge with gratitude the kind efforts of Linda Adeboye, May Mbu and Aishah Ahmad who lent their support and time with the proofreading, selection and editing of many articles before they went to press. I thank Damola Ifaturoti of AMV, my publisher who stood by patiently, and gently encouraged me to remain focused on ensuring that this project was successfully executed.

Special thanks to my husband, Yinka and our three lovely children for their consistent support, and to my siblings, for their constructive criticism, useful comments and ideas.

Above all, I thank God for his guidance and for the gift of writing which made it possible for me to formulate my thoughts and ideas into a meaningful written form. It is my hope that readers will find knowledge and guidance through the words that I share.

Nimi AKINKUGBE

INTRODUCTION

Our lives are shaped by many different life events — some exciting and happy, and some very difficult to endure. Wherever you stand at this moment in time, planning ahead will help you enjoy the good times and better equip you to cope with the more challenging ones. Life's big events, good, bad, happy or sad, come with financial consequences.

The finer details of your personal finances will change as you start out and move from your 20s and 30s to your 40s and 50s and beyond, but the general principles remain the same. The various stages of life are punctuated by significant milestones such as, starting a first job, to getting married and starting a family, educating your children, losing a job, relocating, buying a home, caring for aging parents, losing a loved one, and planning for your retirement and your estate. Too many of us get swept up in such events without being prepared financially. By planning ahead of such events, some of which can be anticipated, you can help preserve and protect your present lifestyle.

The purpose of this book is to remove the mystique surrounding savings and investments and dispel the misconceptions attached to them, while providing readers with concise information and tips on matters concerning the management of their money.

This text takes you on a journey that embraces an extensive and varied range of issues related to personal financial management. *A-Z Of Personal Finance* involves every aspect of your life that involves money; your personal financial situation can affect your relationships, your lifestyle and standard of living and even your perception of yourself.

The *A-Z Of Personal Finance* is a collection of topics, words and terms that we associate with the subject of personal finance. It provides a comprehensive guide and walks readers through their finances as they pass through the various stages of life from childhood, through their careers, retirement and beyond. I have focused on some of the most significant principles in my saving and investing philosophy.

No matter how little or how much money you have or make, no matter how old or young you are, whether you are just starting to build your finances from scratch or are already an experienced investor, I have included strategies to monitor your spending and help you to live within your means, to cope with the burden of debt, navigate the family finances, plan adequately for your children's education and your retirement through regular saving and investing. I have also shared thoughts regarding leaving a lasting legacy for your heirs.

There is no short cut to financial independence. Unless you are lucky enough to win the lottery or happen to inherit a fortune, you will have to build your financial future systematically with careful planning, so don't spend all your time looking to "get rich quick". The key to securing your financial future is about taking many small disciplined steps over a long period of time. It is about having a plan, and a plan requires commitment, determination, discipline, consistency and time.

Nimi AKINKUGBE

FOREWORD

Nimi Akinkugbe is an advocate of financial literacy and education, and has enlightened us over the years regarding the importance of personal financial responsibility and money management through articles, speaking engagements, radio and TV appearances.

Her first book, *A-Z Of Personal Finance,* is a treasure for the youth, parents, teachers, counsellors, mentors, and professionals. This book integrates insights regarding the social and emotional characteristics of spending. Nimi has a unique flair for simplifying complex issues regarding personal financial management and through this book has carefully helped you organise your personal financial matters into categories.

Whilst there are numerous books offering advice about personal finances, *Nimi's A–Z…* stands out as one that clearly benefits from her successful banking career spanning 23 years, which provided her with unique insights into private wealth and asset management. She has consolidated this experience and made it accessible to the reader by presenting information that is both instructive and easy to understand. The introduction at the start of the book sets the tone clearly:

> *"The key to securing your financial future is about taking many small disciplined steps over a long period of time. It is about having a plan, and a plan requires commitment, determination, discipline, consistency and time."*

Nimi writes in a style that is non-judgmental, instructive, and positive. This book provides effective tips and strategies that can help one develop their path to wealth creation and financial security.

I commend this book to you.

Fola ADEOLA, OFR
Co-Founder, Guaranty Trust Bank, Plc
and Chairman, FATE Foundation

A

Asset Allocation

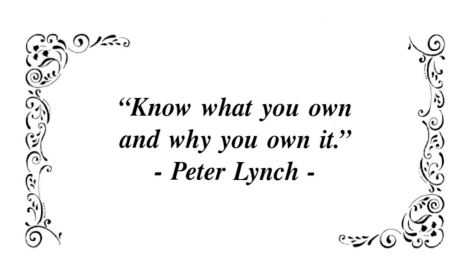

*"Know what you own
and why you own it."*
- Peter Lynch -

Asset Allocation

We've all heard the phrase, "Don't put all your eggs in one basket!" This old maxim perfectly describes the concept of asset allocation. If you put all your savings in one type of investment and the investment fails, you might jeopardise your savings. Asset allocation refers to how you spread your money between a number of different asset classes such as cash, bonds, stocks and real estate. This strategy looks at your particular goals and circumstances and determines the most appropriate asset mix for you within the various asset classes.

The main purpose of this strategy is to reduce investment risk. History has shown that in general, various types of investments perform differently. Whilst money market investments tend to offer relatively low returns, your initial investment is safe. Bonds may not be as lucrative but offer more stability than stocks; they offer a middle ground between cash and stocks in terms of risk and return. Stocks, on the other hand, offer the highest return among these three classes, but they also carry the highest risk. It is thus advisable that an investor's portfolio be divided amongst the various categories.

How Much Should You Put Where?

As you pass through your life cycle, your financial goals will change. Each investor's approach to asset allocation will differ and depend largely upon his or her age, life stage, financial goals and risk tolerance. Generally, the younger you are, the more risk you can afford to take. A 22-year old just starting out in the workforce will have a completely different view of risk from a 55-year old approaching retirement. The closer you are to retirement the more important it is to preserve the wealth that you have worked so hard to accumulate.

Whilst it is true that stocks and real estate offer attractive returns over the long term, they can suffer significant declines. This makes them somewhat unsuitable for investing money that may be needed within, say, the next two to three years. As you approach retirement you want to protect a portfolio from volatility, as a large decline in a portfolio could significantly affect the planned retirement lifestyle or standard of living.

Some General Rules

General rules for asset allocation suggest that any money you need next year should be in cash, money you need in two to three years in fixed-income investments and money you can afford to put away for four to five years and beyond can be invested in the stock market. This ensures that the cash you need today is readily available, that the money you need in a few years time will be safe from stock market volatility and that money you can afford to put away for several years is invested in the stock market.

Another useful rule of thumb is to subtract your age from 100 and invest at least that percentage in stocks. An 80 year old, for example, might be advised to hold only a small portion of, say, 20 percent in stocks whilst the balance is left in cash. A 45 year old on the other hand, might have a portfolio that has 55 percent in stocks and the remaining 45 percent in bonds and cash. Some would suggest that this is too low, particularly where you are saving for retirement which could still be over 20 years away.

Diversification

In many ways asset allocation is synonymous with diversification. In addition to diversifying across asset classes or even geographically, you should also be diversified within each asset class. There are different types of investments within an asset class. For example, when it comes to investing in stocks, instead of investing all your money in just one or two companies you may choose to invest in different sectors including banking, manufacturing, or insurance. This helps you diversify your investment risk, as any losses caused by the downturn in one sector may be offset by a rise in another; it is unlikely that all sectors will perform in exactly the same way and decline at the same time unless there is a general reversal of the entire market. Asset managers generally seek to ensure that no single asset represents more than say 5 to 6 percent of your total portfolio.

Diversify According to Your Goals

Your various goals may require different levels of liquidity. For your short-term goals, such as the funding of a family holiday or a family wedding, this year or the next, you will require cash to make payments. For the longer-term goals such as the funding of your children's education or your retirement, your investments in the stock market or real estate will offer you better prospects for long-term growth.

Asset allocation is a critical part of the process of building a solid investment portfolio. Indeed, various studies have suggested that asset allocation is a major determinant of long-term investment performance.

Bear in mind that asset allocation does not assure you of profit nor does it protect you from losses in a declining market. It is thus important to review your asset allocation strategy periodically and adjust your portfolio as your circumstances and objectives change. This will ensure that the portfolio remains reflective of your long-term needs and outlook whilst also addressing your short and medium term goals. Most of us do not have the time or expertise to manage our finances ourselves; it is thus useful to seek professional advice, as a financial advisor will carefully look at your own unique circumstances and design a portfolio mix that is the most appropriate for you.

B

The Boomerang Generation

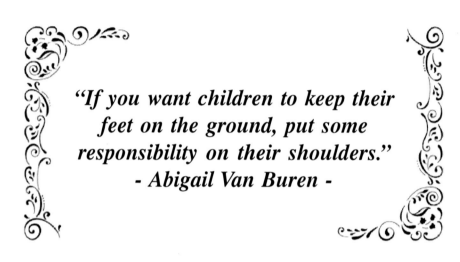

"If you want children to keep their feet on the ground, put some responsibility on their shoulders."
- Abigail Van Buren -

The Boomerang Generation

"The Boomerang Generation" — The Return of the Children

Middle age is usually considered a life stage where you experience the "empty nest syndrome" as children leave home. For many people in their 50s, this has not been the reality; a growing number of "returnees," dubbed the "boomerang generation," are postponing the traditional expectations of leaving home and returning to their childhood bedrooms.

Parental empty nests are filling up with one or more young adults per household whose expensive education thus far has not equipped them to assume the expected next step; moving to their own place and finding a job that provides enough money for them to support themselves.

Why do they Return?

The "boomerang generation" is largely returning home as a matter of necessity. In the current economic climate, most have little choice but to turn to relations or friends for a place to live on the cheap. The job market is bleak, with unemployment on the increase, low salaries for entry-level jobs and the escalating cost of accommodation, making it difficult for young people to be able to rent let alone own their own property soon after they graduate.

It is also true that nowadays parents have become more indulgent. Many have provided a comfortable lifestyle for their children, who are now used to a certain quality of life, a pampered existence that they cannot maintain without claiming it at home. Coming home thus provides an extremely appealing and viable alternative that usually comes free or at least heavily subsidised, with room, meals, utilities and transportation provided.

The Implications

This change in the pattern of life's stages can lead to delayed independence. Indeed, parents may actually be holding their children back from success and a fulfilling life by overindulging them. Naturally many young people would rather keep their options open and are not willing to compromise and accept just any first or entry-level job. Unfortunately, they tend to ignore the need for saving and investing but are often more pre-occupied with the now and instant gratification.

Obviously there are also significant financial implications for parents who themselves have retired or are approaching retirement. The limited funds they have accumulated to be able to enjoy a secure and comfortable retirement after so many years of sacrifice for their children are now being spent on grown-up children.

Plan Ahead

There is the very real possibility that one or more of your children may return home for a while, so as you make projections as to the level of income you may require to sustain your retirement, keep this in mind; this will inevitably raise your monthly outlay or could even delay your retirement plans. In your 40s or 50s, it is likely that you simultaneously have to bear the additional costs of caring for aging parents, continue to support your children and fund your own retirement.

Do not Jeopardise Your Retirement

It is tempting to put aside your own retirement needs for your adult children. To be able to help your family you first need to have some level of financial security. Although you may feel somewhat cash strapped from paying off your mortgage, raising and educating children, and perhaps shouldering some of the costs of care for your parents, be careful not to jeopardise your retirement savings; try to continue to budget, save and keep any debt under control so that you can retain your independence in your retirement years.

Set Some Parameters

If you have "boomerang" children, have a conversation to lay out terms or a broad understanding that sets clear parameters. In some cultures, parents go so far as to draw up a formal contract to outline expectations and financial responsibilities. It is easy for children to slip back into the routine they had before they left home several years ago; but you should encourage them to contribute in some way towards the upkeep of the house, which might include contributing towards weekly groceries, utilities, petrol, diesel and cable TV if they are employed. If you can afford it, set this money aside in savings for them as a small nest egg for the time they eventually leave home. If they are not earning, they could contribute in non-monetary ways such as sharing some of the maintenance and cleaning tasks.

Encourage your children to make a clear financial plan to help them develop sound financial habits that will last them a lifetime. They should endeavour to make specific progress towards budgeting, controlling their debt and saving. Even whilst they are still under your wing, they can learn some harsh lessons about the real world as they navigate the transition from parental dependence to financial independence.

Cashless Society

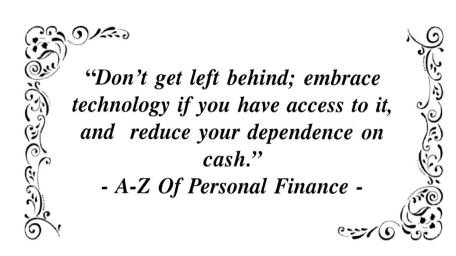

"Don't get left behind; embrace technology if you have access to it, and reduce your dependence on cash."

- A-Z Of Personal Finance -

Cashless Society

Are You Prepared for a Cashless Society?

Are we heading towards a cashless society, where digital or electronic money eventually replaces physical money? The world of banking and finance has been one of the greatest beneficiaries of technological innovation and advancement in global payment systems. The greatest impact has been felt in the actual way transactions take place, that is, the use of physical money itself.

In some developed countries consumers can do almost entirely without the use of hard cash, and electronic means of payments far outstrip cash transactions in much of the industrialised world today; indeed you may be greeted with consternation should you wish to make a purchase with large amounts of cash. Financial institutions are implementing electronic payments via internet banking and plastic cards; credit cards, debit and automatic teller machine (ATM) cards instead of hard cash.

How would you feel if you were told that you would no longer be able to use paper money and would have to rely on electronic technology for all your consumer and financial transactions? We all like the speed and convenience of electronic commerce, but we also like the look and feel of our hard cash; you withdraw cash at the ATM and have a rough idea of how long it will last, you can see what you are spending it on even though it might disappear faster than you intended. Paper money is tangible and feels real and it gives you a sense of really owning something.

All over the world, the trend has been for governments and financial institutions to pursue policies to reduce the volume of cash in the system. No one will be exempt and indeed you cannot afford to be left behind in this initiative. There are many benefits from doing away with "old-fashioned cash." Governments will embrace it, as it is a means of curbing money laundering and other financial crimes, security challenges and the exorbitant cost of cash management to the banking industry. Businesses will embrace it as a means of receiving instant payment and automating their inventory and accounting systems, cutting their expenses and thereby increasing their revenues. Consumers should embrace electronic and internet banking for the speed, convenience, security and efficiency that it provides.

Have You Embraced Internet Banking?

The internet has revolutionised banking and personal finance in many ways. If you have not yet embraced your bank's internet banking service, there are some compelling reasons to do so.

Nowadays, we are all so busy in our professional lives, that there often isn't enough time to visit the bank. With internet banking, you can carry out most of your routine banking transactions at your convenience. If you have internet access, you have unlimited access to your bank accounts; you can check your account balances, pay bills, make transfers and manage your various accounts with a few simple clicks from your laptop or computer, your iPad, or your cell phone.

Do You Routinely Use Debit Cards or Credit Cards?

Your debit card electronically transfers funds from your bank account to the store where you are making a purchase. You do not need to visit your bank each time you need to withdraw money, as an increasing number of merchants, including shops, restaurants, clubs etc, will accept your debit card. This means that you do not have to carry cash and risk having it stolen.

While a credit card is advantageous because purchases can typically be paid back over time, interest rates, which usually exceed 20 percent per year, tend to create significant debt, depending on how much the consumer spends on credit card purchases. It is thus important to be cautious and disciplined with a credit card.

As nations take bold steps to implement change and modernise their economies, naturally they will face obstacles. The wide acceptability of card-based transactions and easy access to the internet makes it possible for these initiatives to take root quickly in developed economies. For most developing countries, however, there is still some way to go for a cashless society to become a reality. This however does not prevent individuals from starting to adapt their behaviour accordingly.

How prepared are you for change? It is important to begin to become familiar with the alternative electronic payment channels available to you and decide which will best suit your personal financial habits. Don't get left behind; embrace technology if you have access to it and reduce your dependence on cash.

C

Conspicuous Consumption

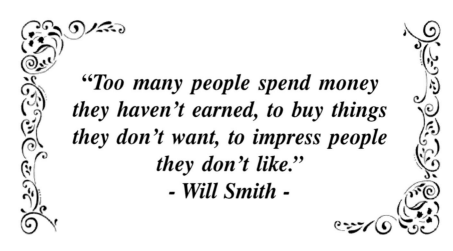

"Too many people spend money they haven't earned, to buy things they don't want, to impress people they don't like."
- Will Smith -

Conspicuous Consumption

I n 1899 economist and sociologist Thorstein Veblem coined the phrase "conspicuous consumption" in his book *The Theory of the Leisure Class* (1899). He argued that some consumption is intended to send a message about the consumers' status rather than just to satisfy a need. "Consumers buy certain goods because of what those goods reveal about their standing in society, rather than the intrinsic enjoyment they derive from the purchase." Conspicuous consumption is the ostentatious display and the consumption of resources by the wealthy class, in particular, to advertise their wealth.

With the growing prosperity in some segments of society, we are continually seeking ways to outdo each other by showing off and boasting. As the term "keeping up with the Joneses" suggests, we measure our success against those around us and have become so consumed with the image of affluence that we fail to be content with the pleasure and satisfaction that comes from financial stability and good old-fashioned family values.

The Impact of Conspicuous Consumption

The impact of conspicuous consumption has several negative effects that include serious societal implications. The upsurge in incidents of violence is not an isolated phenomenon; it portrays a complex set of political, cultural and social trends that prevail in the polity. Cultural and religious intolerance are often cited among the catalysts to unrest, and certainly these must be addressed, but unless remedied, the strong underlying economic factors that fuel violence, will continue unabated and can create irreparable damage to economic development.

The wide and ever widening abyss in incomes between the rich and poor and the incredible show of opulence and ostentatious living by the rich slowly give rise to a sense of despondency, deprivation and degradation among much of the populace that largely lives in abject poverty. Most people at the short end of the economic divide are resigned to their fate and appear to accept their lot, but a small minority becomes restive and translates its resentment and wrath into acts of violence and disorder.

All over the world such resentment breeds a desperation that can become extreme and manifest in organised political resistance or sectarian violence that could eventually result in lawlessness, armed robbery, murder, assassination and other extreme acts of violence. Conspicuous spending sends a powerful message to a society, and particularly to impressionable youths, that they must strive to make money by hook or by crook. On the contrary, they must be encouraged to value education, hard work, ambition and ability and to realise that, given the opportunity, they can and will succeed by dint of sheer hard work and perseverance.

Financial, Social and Economic Discipline

Financing items or activities that have little or no real value can drastically affect your economic security. Such audacious spending diverts funds away from saving and investing. The "play now, pay later" syndrome implies that people who spend a large part of their wealth on acquiring luxuries, often on credit, are in essence robbing their retirement funds and could ultimately undermine their future financial security.

Stop comparing yourself to others! There will always be people that simply have much, much more than you can ever hope to have; nicer homes, cars, clothes, jewelry. If you are constantly trying to outdo them - and remember you don't know how they attained their wealth - you will put yourself under intense pressure and undermine your financial wellbeing. It is wiser to examine your own particular situation and look at ways of improving yourself, for example, through self-development and education. Focus on what is really important to you. It is tempting to imitate others and want what they have, but if you stay focused on your own goals, chances are that you won't be distracted.

The phenomenon of wasteful and lavish consumption to enhance social prestige can be reversed where the mindset shifts towards a disciplined approach to wealth creation and spending, where there is a systematic approach to achieving long-term financial goals and being less swayed by short-term impressions and wants.

For many of us today, this realisation often comes far too late. Unfortunately, a growing number of people are living far beyond their means in an effort to impress others. Some people "appear" to be wealthy; making a feverish display of opulence and wealth that sometimes shields huge liabilities and debt.

There is a discipline associated with creating, building and retaining true wealth; it comes from saving and investing wisely and maintaining a disciplined mindset and a cautious approach to spending. Acquiring and maintaining long-term wealth is a process with few short cuts, but the rewards over time are well beyond the thrill of any instant gratification or outward image.

D

Debt

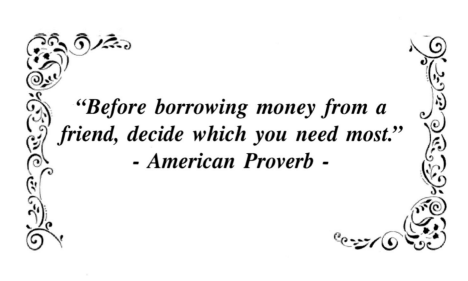

"Before borrowing money from a friend, decide which you need most."
- American Proverb -

Debt

Are you facing money problems? The early warning signs are usually very clear and include the following:

- You are completely broke long before payday
- You are regularly having to borrow from friends and relations just to make ends meet
- You are missing debt payments
- You are coming under pressure from lenders
- Your money worries are keeping you awake at night

So how did you get to this point? Is it your lifestyle? Are you extravagant? Do you make poor spending decisions? Are you trying to keep up socially? Perhaps you are just not earning enough to fund your lifestyle and obligations. There are so many reasons for money problems, but the good news is that it is possible to turn your financial life around.

By recognising and acknowledging the fact that there is indeed a problem, you can start to take the deliberate and necessary steps to address it.

Your attitude to your debt problems can hinder your financial recovery. If your way of dealing with it is to wish it away, remember that inaction will only make things worse. With interest, late payment penalty charges, and the attendant fees and charges you will find that almost all your money goes towards debt service. It is important to get your debt under control and aim to clear or at least reduce it significantly.

Make a List of all Your Debts

Who do you owe? How much do you owe? What is the interest rate on your loan? To get a true picture of what you owe, list all your debts - in no particular order at first. You can list them according to amount, due dates, interest rates, the creditors you owe – it doesn't really matter. It is important to know how much debt you owe if you are going to get out of it.

Be sure that you are current with the minimum payments on all your debt. If you are not, contact your creditors to discuss your payments. It may be possible to restructure the debt in a way that enables you to repay in amounts you can afford. Failure to make timely payments will only make things worse, and your loan interest will accumulate.

Create a Budget

Track your expenses for a month to determine exactly what comes in and what you are spending it on. Determine how much you need to spend on food, transport, clothing, school fees, entertainment, utilities and housing and then set strict spending limits. There is usually some waste lurking in the monthly budget; be realistic and honest with yourself, as you must find a way to cut back. If you can find just that little bit of extra money after budgeting for your essential expenses, then you can use this towards reducing your debt.

Make every effort to stop the bleeding and try not to incur any additional debt. It is tempting to continue to use your credit card(s) to make additional payments but consider the fact that the smallest payments add up and increase your debt. Naturally you may have to live below your comfort level for a time and will certainly have to do without some luxuries, but it will be well worth it in the end.

Prioritise Your Debt

Put your bills in the order in which you want to pay them off. Ideally it should be organised according to interest rates. It makes sense to pay off high-interest debt first, as this will maximise your debt payments and reduce the amount of overall interest that you pay. Ultimately, the higher the rate, the more you're paying beyond your actual principal. Some people prefer to start by paying off their smallest debts first, as this quickly gives a sense of achievement and can provide a significant boost as you systematically pay off your debts.

Bear in mind that the most important debts aren't necessarily the largest. These are the ones where serious action can be taken against you if you don't pay what you owe such as rent or mortgage repayments, secured loans and utility bills. If you don't sort these out, you will be disconnected from utilities, face eviction or the repossession of your home. As you start to tackle your "priority" debts, determine how much extra you can afford to pay each month over and above the minimum monthly repayments.

The Faces of Debt: The Good, The Bad and The Ugly

It is almost impossible to live totally debt-free; most people will borrow money at some stage in their lives. Borrowing can be a useful way to help spread out the cost of large purchases or expenses that you could perhaps not otherwise afford. It can also help you through difficult times or periods when there just isn't enough cash to go around. Borrowing to invest can make it possible to attain greater levels of financial success than if one depends solely on ones own resources. Debt often has negative connotations, ignoring the fact that there is a difference between "good debt" and "bad debt".

"Good Debt" vs "Bad Debt"

"Good debt" is debt that creates value and can help to build wealth and generate income. This includes borrowing to buy property, to finance an education, a business or for investment purposes such as for the purchase of property or shares.

"Bad debt" is where you borrow to finance lifestyle purchases such as clothes, jewellery, expensive cars, holidays, or just to have a good time; these are expenses that should ideally be paid for in cash and not with credit cards and personal loans. Bad debt does not usually generate income or wealth. Resist borrowing to buy things that will quickly depreciate.

Debt has become a necessary part of life for most people but should be viewed as a tool to help you attain your financial goals. Using credit responsibly should help build wealth, provide greater opportunities and enhance your quality of life; yet for those who have borrowed excessively and for the wrong reasons, debt can have dire consequences. Sometimes it makes sense to borrow; sometimes it doesn't. Do give yourself some credit, but be careful.

E

Education Planning — Part 1

"Your children's education is likely to be your greatest priority, but do not neglect your own retirement plans. If these fall short, you may find yourself financially dependent on your children."
- A-Z Of Personal Finance -

Education Planning – Part 1

Planning for Your Children's Education

Naturally it is the desire of every parent or guardian to give their children the best possible start in life. One of the best ways to build a foundation for a secure future is to provide him or her with a sound education. Education opens doors to many opportunities, and is a necessity in today's global economy. For you and the vast majority of people, funding your children's education ranks as one of the largest expenses you will ever incur and it must thus be carefully planned for.

Start Saving Now

If your children are still babies or toddlers, thinking about their future education may seem like a lifetime away. However, given the rising costs of education, the earlier you start making financial provision for this most important goal, the better. Certainly, the most difficult time to start an education savings plan is when your children are still young, which can be a challenge for new parents who are just starting to build assets and to face the financial demands of a young family. However, this is the time to start saving in earnest.

Unless you are very well off financially, it may be difficult to suddenly have to come up with the money to pay for your children's secondary or tertiary education when it is time for them to go. Prepare for these costs now rather than later; even if you can't put aside a large sum each month from the onset, start with a small amount, and increase it whenever you can. With a head start, your funds will have time to appreciate and weather the inevitable ups and downs of the financial markets.

It is true that most advice on education funding focuses on building a savings plan early. This would be ideal, but even if your children are older and you haven't been saving for their education, it's never too late to take steps to ease this burden and improve their prospects.

How Much Can You Afford to Set Aside on a Regular Basis?

The amount of money you can set aside is a function of how much you can afford. Consider the assets you hold, your debt situation and what you can realistically save given all your other commitments. Your neighbour may be able to deposit a large monthly sum into their child's education fund; this may not be possible for you. Don't be tempted to copy others. Look at your family's unique financial circumstances and determine what makes sense for you; what you can afford and can stay committed to for the long-term.

Automate your savings via direct debit from your current account to an appropriate savings vehicle. This "forced" saving method will help you keep your plans on track. The key is to keep making steady, regular progress until your children complete their studies.

How Much Does it Cost Now?

In planning for your children's education you must estimate what the total cost is likely to be. It is better to overestimate than to risk having a shortfall that might affect your plans later on. Major expenses include tuition fees, accommodation, textbooks, computers, sporting equipment, uniforms, transportation, extracurricular activities, private tutors and personal expenses. Even though the numbers will not be firm, having some estimates will help you to keep your goals in view.

Begin to determine the type of school you are aiming for. Tuition fees vary enormously between state and private schools, and there is a wide range within each category; so do some research regarding prices.

How Much Will it Cost in the Future?

By some estimates, annual increases in education costs range between 10 percent and 15 percent each year. Bear in mind that actual percentage increases in any given year might be significantly higher or lower and that rates might vary between public and private colleges. In any case, this means that children born today will face a tuition bill or student loan several times more than the average student pays today.

Factor in how much prices have risen historically year after year to help you make financial projections. On the internet there are numerous savings calculators that can help you visualise various scenarios, for example, by assuming a monthly or quarterly deposit of "X" amounts, over a period of "Y" years and applying an interest rate of "Z" percent, you will be able to determine the total yield at a future date. You will also need to factor in exchange rate changes if it is your intention for your children to be educated abroad.

Play with the numbers a little to see what happens when you earn a higher interest rate on your deposit or if you miss a month's payment or are able to make an extra payment. A financial calculator will help you determine how much to put into the education fund each month in order to meet a particular goal. For many families there might be more than one child to consider, so multiply the cost estimates accordingly, and see the effect this will have on the overall plan.

As you prepare financially for your children's education, remember that while you want your offspring to succeed in life, you don't want to drain all your savings and jeopardise your own financial plans, planning for your retirement. Try to find a happy medium between selecting a school that is not only affordable, but also offers a sound education.

E

Education Planning — Part 2

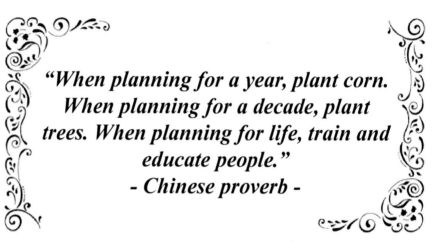

"When planning for a year, plant corn. When planning for a decade, plant trees. When planning for life, train and educate people."
- Chinese proverb -

Education Planning – Part 2

Save Now or You'll Pay Later

Many parents pay school fees on an ad hoc basis without any advance planning. With the rising cost of education, if sound investments are not made now, covering the huge expenses for the secondary and post-secondary years may be a challenge. When your children are still young, you have the benefit of time to select investments that offer the prospect of higher returns. In addition, compounding provides the advantage of additional earnings on the interest and the capital gains on your investment.

What are Your Options?

Consider the available options, and identify the risks involved in each before investing. Money market deposits offer you a low risk option, but the returns hardly keep pace with inflation. In order to accumulate enough money to afford educational costs in the years ahead, you need to not only start early, but to invest fairly aggressively. Given past experiences, many people are still nervous about investing in the stock market, yet it is generally regarded as the best option for long-term investing; in the short term it can be volatile. If your time frame covers a ten-year period, you may consider investing a significant part of the money in the stock market. An equity fund will offer you diversification by spreading your capital across a carefully selected range of stocks.

As the time draws closer, minimising your risk and preserving your capital takes precedence over the prospect of high returns. It makes sense to begin to shift the funds into more conservative investments such as bonds and then money market assets to carefully secure the fees when they fall due; you would thus have gradually moved away from the volatility and risk of stocks toward the lower volatility of bonds and the relative safety of money market assets. If you leave the money in the stock market till just before the time you need it, you may be forced to sell stocks at a loss.

Do You Have Any Assets?

Real estate is an asset class that performs well in certain locations. It provides three main sources of funds; you can sell some or all of your property, you can apply the rental income to pay tuition and other costs, or you can release part of your equity.

It is only the highly paid or well off who can afford to fund the full cost of tuition upfront. For the vast majority of people, additional sources of funding are required. Unsecured loans can be made available for high-income earners in full-time employment, but it is more common to secure a loan against your property or other high-value assets. You may be eligible to borrow a percentage of your equity, which is the difference between the market value of your property and the outstanding mortgage loan. Be cautious as you consider debt, for paying interest on a loan can significantly increase your overall education costs; and if you default, you could lose your property.

Scholarships

Scholarships and grants are often overlooked by parents as a source of education funding. From your children's earliest years you may have identified a unique skill or talent, or they may be exceptionally gifted academically, making them eligible to compete for a scholarship. Nurture their talent and seek to develop it; at the same time, be careful not to push them too hard, as you might be demanding a performance level from your children that they may not yet be capable of producing which may lead to frustration.

Scholarships sometimes have strings attached and may be tied to a particular field of study or may require that a certain standard of performance be maintained. They often cover less than half of the total costs, so you will still have to come up with the difference.

Will Your Children Have to Contribute?

For many families it is the norm and an economic necessity that children contribute towards the funding of their university education by working full-time and taking advantage of distance learning opportunities outside their immediate environment or by enrolling in part-time courses. It is important that you teach them economic responsibility when they are young as their earnings can supplement whatever you are able to provide towards their living expenses. By encouraging them to invest in their own education, you will also be teaching invaluable lessons in personal financial management.

Keep Your Retirement Plans in View

Your children's education is likely to be your greatest priority, but do not neglect your own retirement plans. If these fall short, you may find yourself financially dependent on your children. Do not be tempted to withdraw money from your retirement savings account other than for your retirement, as it could jeopardise your ability to maintain your own future financial independence.

Insurance is available to protect your children's education. Tuition-protection plans are designed to provide you with the peace of mind of knowing that their education will be secure and can continue unhampered in the event of a loss of employment, permanent disability, or the demise of the parent or sponsor.

It is important to bear in mind that there is no one solution; each investor's circumstances are different. Seek professional advice. An investment advisor will carefully consider your own unique family circumstances and goals and assist you in making the most appropriate decision, taking into account your income, your children's age, your risk tolerance, your investment time horizon and the amount you wish to save. With a disciplined and systematic approach to investing over time, you will be able to accumulate a significant sum in your children's education fund. The sooner you start investing the better.

E

Estate Planning

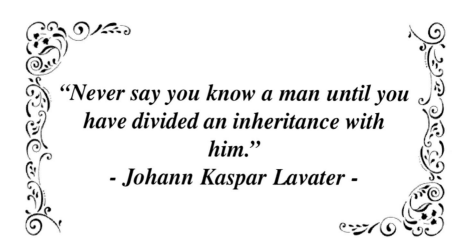

"*Never say you know a man until you have divided an inheritance with him.*"
- *Johann Kaspar Lavater* -

Estate Planning

"We're dividing all of mother's things,
Deciding on her rugs and rings
I can't believe what's happening tonight.
Can't split a painting on a wall
Or share a table in the hall.
I never dreamt that we could fall apart,
It would break our mother's heart.
Tonight, we're in a family fight.
And yet as kids we'd talk away the night.
But now, we're in a family fight."
—Les Kotzer, *The Family Fight*

Look around you; look at your wonderful close-knit family. Can you imagine that in 20 years your children might not even be talking to each other? These were siblings who once laughed together, played together and shared everything having grown up in the same home. It may seem unthinkable, but if your legacy does matter to you, tidy up your affairs now.

Misunderstandings may arise over the disposition of personal effects and possessions, especially where they have strong sentimental value. Relatively inexpensive objects become the focus of cherished memories. Something as simple as a father's special chair or a mother's cherished rug or jewelry can suddenly have connotations as family heirlooms with powerful links to childhood memories. Where significant financial assets and real estate are involved, the stakes are even higher and the ensuing bitterness often splits families apart.

Families have become more fragmented and complex, with divorces, multiple marriages and children from different households. Such disruptions have inevitably led to complicated bequests and a greater potential for conflict. In addition, the combination of the steep drop in stock prices and the decline in real estate values have been cited as having contributed to an increase in acrimony and family feuds sometimes even leading to litigation.

There are a few issues to consider that can help to minimise potential conflict over the family estate:

Do Not Procrastinate

It is important to plan for your estate before you are unable to do so. If you never get around to tidying up your affairs, you may be compounding the difficulty that your beneficiaries will experience after you are gone. It is often a reluctance to address our mortality or a feeling that the time isn't quite right that causes such procrastination. Ideally, anyone who has assets and who has a spouse or children should make a will as early as possible, even in their 30s and 40s.

Organise Your Financial Records

Keeping track of all of your financial information and maintaining it in an organised way is vital. The stress of pawing through someone else's disorganised records and documents can make an already trying situation unbearable. Bank statements, insurance documents, tax returns and brokerage accounts should all be carefully filed.

Get a Good Lawyer

Discuss your options with an experienced estate planning lawyer who will consider the most appropriate estate planning tool for you; from trusts to lifetime gifts and, of course, your will. Make sure your will is current, as this remains one of the most important instruments for the orderly, peaceful disposition of your assets.

It is important that your will be carefully drafted, as imprecise, ambiguous language can cause confusion; if sensitive family dynamics are not carefully considered, relatives may still feud. It can be difficult to determine what is fair, and often, in an effort to divide assets fairly, parents create what has been referred to as "inadvertent inequality."

Consider this scenario:

Mr. Coker willed the following properties indiscriminately to his three children:
- A block of 4 apartments to the eldest child
- A warehouse on a half-acre plot to the second child
- A 4-bedroom house on one acre of prime real estate to the youngest child

The two older siblings felt "hard done by" and are fighting their younger sibling over the higher property in one of the best parts of the city.

Pick the Right Executor and Trustees

Select an executor that you believe can carry out your wishes effectively. It is possible for qualified family members to serve as executors, but if you feel the potential for sibling conflict is real, consider appointing a trusted outsider, or a professional body to perform this important task. In another scenario, Mr. Babson left all his assets to his second wife, expecting that she would pass on assets as appropriate to his son. She bequeathed everything to her own children. Her stepson did not receive anything and is going to court. After a remarriage, a trust might be more appropriate for the protection of new beneficiaries such as a second spouse or for children from an earlier marriage.

Some other special circumstances can create potential disagreements in the disposition of assets. For example, an adult child might have spent several years caring for a parent, perhaps even giving up a career to do so; the parent might thus wish to express gratitude with a special monetary gift.

There could be an irresponsible child or one who has an addiction that could decimate an inheritance; some parents may be tempted to disinherit that child. Such a decision should be carefully weighed, as this could lead to acrimony within the family. A trust vehicle is particularly useful in this regard, as trustees can manage and disburse funds on behalf of any child; an option most suited to accommodate special situations.

Sort Out Issues Relating to Your Assets Title

Many disputes arise as a result of assets being transferred during a parent's lifetime out of convenience or other reasons, often bypassing the will. An aging parent may require some assistance with their finances and provide a child with access to bank and investment accounts. Setting up such joint accounts may, however, conflict with the provisions of a will.

Some people opt for a gifting strategy and give away certain assets during their lifetime. Observing how beneficiaries handle lifetime gifts can lend important insights as to how future inheritance might be handled.

Letter of Instruction

In addition to a will there is a less formal document that provides information for family members in the event of death or incapacitation.

In a letter of instruction you can include the name of key professionals to be contacted such as your banker, accountant, insurance agent and stockbroker, as well as the location of important documents such as wills, insurance policies and title documents. Information about any debt, such as a mortgage can also be included.

Even though it does not have any legal authority and is not a will substitute, a letter of instruction serves a very useful purpose in that it clearly articulates your overall intention for your estate to your executor. It can be as personal as you wish and can also be used to send important messages to children and grandchildren as to your expectations of them and the important values you want to pass on.

The loss of a parent is always a trying time, and unfortunately it can bring out the worst in siblings at a time when they need their parent's wise counsel more than ever. With careful thought and planning and, most importantly, professional advice, you can mitigate much of the potential conflict and leave a lasting legacy.

F

Family Finances

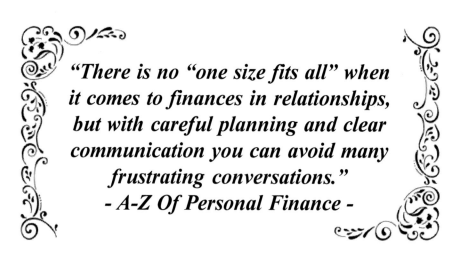

"There is no "one size fits all" when it comes to finances in relationships, but with careful planning and clear communication you can avoid many frustrating conversations."
- A-Z Of Personal Finance -

Family Finances

Yours, Mine and Ours

As two individuals merge all their worldly goods, there are many things to consider. After the excitement of the wedding ceremonies, it is time to face your financial future together. Have you effected your name change on your documents? Will you have joint or separate accounts? How will you manage your investments? Have you updated your insurance policies to reflect your new beneficiary?

Name Changes

Should you decide to adopt your spouse's name, take time to update your records; change your name on your drivers' license on your share certificates, on your will and other legal documents. Notify your employer, creditors, insurance agents and bankers who will need to see your certified marriage certificate as legal proof of your new status before any changes can be effected.

Review Your Insurance

If you and your spouse work and are covered by separate health plans, through your jobs, compare the two plans as you may find that it might work out cheaper to have one family plan instead of two individual ones. This is a good time to discuss life insurance. When you are single and without dependants, this will not be a priority, but in a marriage, and certainly where one party is the primary breadwinner, a life insurance policy is appropriate, as a sudden loss of income can be devastating to a young family.

Dealing with Debt

Many people don't discover the extent of their spouse's financial obligations until they are married. Debt can be a major source of strife if not disclosed before the marriage. Whilst you are not legally responsible for the credit card debt or other loans opened in your spouse's name, it could affect your eligibility for joint loans such as a mortgage. Even if the debt may have been incurred before the marriage or afterwards or even after a legal separation, try to deal with the debt together and seek to bring it under control.

Separate Accounts, Joint Accounts or a Combination

You may prefer to maintain a certain degree of independence by keeping separate accounts for personal spending. If your partner is a spendthrift whilst you are a saver or you just prefer to spend your money without your partner scrutinising the minutest detail, separate accounts may be more appropriate. Parties to a joint account have a right to withdraw all the money in the account. It is for this reason that the use of joint accounts is usually limited to people who have built a solid level of trust; generally close family members, partners, parents and children. For example, an elderly parent may open a joint account with an adult child to pay household bills or to avoid the complicated probate court process in the event of their demise. A parent may also opt to maintain a joint account with a child to provide immediate access to funds should the need arise.

Having a joint account combined with individual accounts for personal expenses is a good compromise, as each partner takes some responsibility for the household budget yet is still able to retain some autonomy. Partners contribute a certain amount of their monthly salary into the joint account to cover routine household expenses such as food, utility bills, and larger expenses to meet family needs and goals, such as rent or mortgage payments, school fees and family vacations. If one partner earns significantly more or less than the other, it's only fair to contribute amounts in proportion to your respective incomes that reflect this imbalance.

Joint Account Holders and Authorised Signatories

There is sometimes confusion about the difference between a joint account holder and an authorised signatory. Creditors view a joint account as they would an individual account, which means that each account holder is financially liable, and that either party can withdraw funds at will.

It is important to note that whilst an authorised signatory is able to operate the account, the main account holder can choose to remove or change his or her access at any stage. If the main account holder dies, the other signatory to the account would cease to have access to any money because the account would form part of the deceased estate.

Update Your Beneficiaries

It may seem absurd to be discussing your estate plan at this stage of your life, but you need to update the beneficiary designations on your employers "next of kin" form, for your bank accounts, retirement savings account, insurance policies and your will. This is doubly important if this is not your first marriage.

One advantage of a joint account with the "right of survivorship" is that if one of the two joint account holders passes away suddenly the surviving account holder is entitled to the account. Assets such as bank accounts, brokerage accounts and property titled in both your names will usually pass to your spouse or partner without going through the probate process. It is important to consider these issues so that your assets will be divided according to your wishes should something happen to one or both of you. Seek legal advice as to the best way to title your accounts and other property.

There is no "one size fits all" when it comes to finances in relationships, but with careful planning and clear communication you can avoid many frustrating conversations. Even the best system is not always appropriate for your needs so be prepared to modify your system as your relationship and financial situation evolve. If one option doesn't work, try another.

G

Guardian

"Unless you specifically name a guardian in your will, a family member can step forward, and the court will determine who is the most appropriate to perform the role."

- A-Z Of Personal Finance -

G

Guardian

Who will Take Care of Your Kids when You are Gone?

What a horrid thought! Try asking this question to parents and many of them are likely to break into chants of prayer; it is not considered polite to talk about things like that. The writing of a will or any mention of death, almost feels like you are courting or tempting fate.

Deciding on a legal guardian designated to care for your minor children if you pass away, or, worse still, if your spouse or partner passes on as well, is one of the most important decisions you will ever face as a parent. Don't just assume that your extended family social network will make things easy and that your mother or perhaps your brother will automatically receive custody. Unless you specifically name a guardian in your will, a family member can step forward and the court will determine who is the most appropriate to perform the role.

What is the Guardian's Family Situation?

How many children does your candidate already have and what are their ages? It would be ideal if the potential guardian has children of a similar age to yours so that they grow up together. Do you want your child to be raised by a single sibling or friend, a single parent, or a married couple with or without children? There are so many possible scenarios.

Where does the guardian live and is this in line with your plans for your children? The most likely thing to happen is that your children will have to leave their home to move in with the guardian. Can the guardian's home accommodate their family and yours? Will your child have to move far away from familiar friends and surroundings? Will your children be separated? What is most important is that your child be brought up in a warm, nurturing environment that is conducive for a child already traumatised by such terrible loss.

Do the potential Guardian's Values and Beliefs Reflect Yours?

If the potential guardian is already a parent, then you would have already observed the way he or she bring up children. Consider the potential guardian's own background and experiences; does each one's parenting skills, values, and religious beliefs reflect yours? Granted, you may never find someone with exactly the same beliefs and standards as yours, but also consider their faith and views on discipline, ethics, education, sports, music and social values of each candidate. Remember, this is the person who you will be trusting to shape your children's live's in your absence.

How Old is the Guardian?

An older guardian is more likely to be financially secure and thus able to afford to raise your children. Grandparents are often an ideal choice, particularly if they are well and strong, or relatively young; they are also likely to have the time required to properly oversee the child. If the guardian is too old however, their state of health may become an issue and they may become ill or pass away before the children become adults.

If you want your parents to be your children's guardian but fear that they will be too old to manage them as time goes by, you can specify that they be designated guardians for a set period of time after which responsibility can then pass on to a younger person. Be conscious of the fact, however, that a younger guardian, such as an adult sibling, may be a student or may be too involved in beginning a career or starting a family to pay enough attention to your children.

The Guardian and Money Matters

It is important to consider a guardian's financial situation. Practical issues such as the guardian's housing and transport situation, food and clothing, medical expenses and most importantly education must be carefully thought through. Does he or she have a stable job and earn a steady income and can they comfortably cater to the demands of additional mouths to feed?

The situation might be awkward where the guardian is far less well off than you. If the guardian is experiencing financial difficulty or there just isn't enough money to go round, your children might be seen as a burden and the guardian may be tempted to turn to your assets to support the whole family. Financial matters, however, should not necessarily be your primary consideration, and it would be a mistake to eliminate an ideal prospect from the list because you don't think he or she has the financial wherewithal to take care of your children. Remember, it is your responsibility to try to ensure that raising your children does not become a financial strain on the guardian.

One hopes that you have adequate life insurance or have saved and invested and put a will or a trust in place. With proper estate planning whilst you are alive, these issues would have been addressed. A trust can hold assets you pass on to your children. It is a very flexible vehicle and allows you to leave specific instructions as to how trust funds should be applied. The trustee may thus be instructed to provide financial assistance to the guardian to help offset the increased expenses to extend their home or to move to a larger home and pay for other incidentals such as special tuition, medical bills and holidays.

On the other hand, if your children are entitled to much more than the children he or she already lives with, this could also be an issue. For example, your intention may be that your children go to a private school whilst the guardian's children may not. If you can afford it, and the guardian is indeed the ideal choice, you could make some provision in your will, for the guardian's children so that the difference is not too glaring.

The simplest way to deal with money matters would be to give the guardian access to money when needed without having to go back and forth to a third party. Whilst someone might make an ideal guardian, they may not be good with money. It may be that the best home for your children would be with your sister, whilst your father may be the best person to make financial decisions. Ideally, one should have the children's inheritance handled by a professional trustee; such a separation of roles will provide some checks and balances over how the money is spent. Remember to consider how well the guardian and trustee can work together as disagreements may arise from time to time.

Will the Potential Guardian Accept this Responsibility?

Guardianship is a huge responsibility, and not everyone will feel able to take up such a role. Narrow your list down to a few key people, formally ask each one and seek a firm response. As the years go by revisit your estate plan, as the chosen guardian may no longer be appropriate as circumstances change; perhaps that person will have become too old or your relationship might have changed. In your separate wills you and your spouse should name the same person as guardian, and family members should be advised of your decision, to minimise any potential for conflict.

Remember, unless you name a guardian, it will be court's role to appoint a family member who applies and one whom it deems appropriate. Worse still, your children could end up being dumped on someone whom you are not particularly fond of or someone who is not keen on having them.

H

Happiness & Money

"Money can bring happiness but for the most part it is temporary.... It is through generosity that one can attain the best relationship with money. By deciding to make a difference in someone else's life, you give more meaning to your own. The joy that this brings is a lasting form of happiness."
- A-Z Of Personal Finance -

Happiness & Money

Does Money Buy Happiness?

The constant message relayed in our society that money is the most important thing in our lives and the constant desire for more have had far reaching consequences for our societal value system and morals. This unending pursuit of money has damaged family relationships, the environment and global socioeconomic systems.

Sadly, in our consumption-driven society many of us have come to believe that all our worries would be solved if we have more money. Indeed, wealth has become the ultimate measure of who we are, and we have become defined by it. Chasing after money for its own sake can damage our value system and we pay for it in time, health and stress.

What does Money Mean to You?

Do you have a healthy relationship with your money? Do you worship it? Or do you use it as a tool to achieve your goals? Does your life depend on it? What really matters to you? What really does make you feel happy and fulfilled?

It is important to understand your own money personality and to put it in the right perspective. The ways in which you make money and how you spend it reveal a lot about your personality. This relates to the emotional aspects of money such as needs, values, relationship choices, feelings about earning and career choices, spending, saving and investing. Issues of control, security, self-esteem and a sense of well-being are always evident when money matters come up.

Maslow's "Hierarchy of Needs"

What do you need? Abraham Maslow was an American psychologist best known for his theory of the "hierarchy of needs" which he developed in the mid-1900's. This model served as a tool for understanding human motivation and development. He identified five levels of human needs that must be satisfied by one's own environment in order for an individual to reach his or her full potential. Maslow's pyramid illustrates human needs stacked in layers with physiological needs at the base of the pyramid which involves the most basic needs; that is, what a person needs to stay alive, such as air, water, food, sleep, warmth, shelter and hygiene and self-actualisation and fulfilment at the highest level.

The first (and lowest) level involves the most basic needs; that is, what a person needs in order to stay alive such as air, water, food, sleep, warmth, shelter and hygiene. At the second level, Maslow places safety, security, employment, money and financial stability, and good health. By the fifth level the human being seeks self-actualisation and fulfilment. He or she has the desire and the ability to grow; doing something that makes life complete such as supporting a cause or following a calling to realise personal potential or seeking personal growth.

The Relationship Between Money and Happiness

Why doesn't the lucrative promotion or the brand-new five-bedroom house keep us swathed in a permanent state of happiness? We like to think that if we just had a little bit more money, we would be happier, but once we attain that goal, something is still missing. It appears that the more money we have, the more we want; but buying the car, boat, or bike of our dreams will only bring transient joy instead of a deep, lasting sense of fulfilment. We tend to overestimate how much pleasure we will get from having more money.

Certainly, earning more makes us happy in the short term, but we quickly adjust to a new lifestyle and all it brings. Naturally there is a thrill in having that shiny new car, but soon most of us get used to it and start wanting the newer, more powerful model. Having made a special purchase, we immediately dream of acquiring the better, "latest" version. Scientists call it 'the hedonic treadmill' – and many people spend far too much time on it.

"The Hedonic Treadmill"

Professor Emeritus Lord Richard Layard, Director of The Centre for Economic Performance at the London School of Economics, in his book *Happiness: Lessons from the New Science* discusses the relationship between happiness and rising standards of wealth. A critic of consumer society and the all-consuming pursuit of money, he suggests that we eventually get trapped on the "hedonic treadmill": Our happiness begins to wane as we start to take the new positive changes in our life for granted.

Money can bring happiness but for the most part it is temporary. A dramatic change in wealth such as the move from abject poverty to financial security can significantly increase happiness, but satisfaction will be transient; its effect will only last until the beneficiary gets used to the new status. Layard argues that once poverty and discomfort have been eliminated, extra income is much less important than human relationships. So how do we step off that hedonic treadmill?

What Brings More Lasting Happiness?

Having spent several years interacting with people with various levels of wealth, I am convinced that money does not in itself create or sustain happiness. It certainly buys things and improves the quality of life and a standard of living. Yes, money is important, as it helps you to pay your bills, to educate your children, support your family and so on; but if you rely upon it as the key to happiness, it can be illusory as it does not always address life's real issues, such as, concern for your family, problems in relationships and work-related stress.

Money can buy food, shelter, education and experiences, and it pays for healthcare and day-to-day comforts. Of course if you don't have enough money to send your children to school, can't provide for your elderly parents, or can't afford costly surgery that can alleviate the pain from an old injury, it would be hard to be happy. In that sense, money can buy happiness by eliminating some worries and bringing quick relief to financial concerns.

Beyond that, longer-term happiness is dependent upon your personality and on realising how fortunate you are to have the things that truly matter in life: a strong relationship with God, a loving family, good reliable friends, good health for yourself and your loved ones, a fulfilling and secure job, a safe environment, moral values and freedom. Next to these things all the money in the world pales into insignificance.

Happiness Comes from Giving

Having money is a great responsibility because it enables one to do things. Material possessions eventually lose their sparkle then beg to be replaced. Yet, one can make transformational gifts by helping others and even shaping or saving lives. It is through generosity that one can attain the best relationship with money. By deciding to make a difference in someone else's life, you give more meaning to your own. The joy that this brings is a lasting form of happiness.

H

Homes

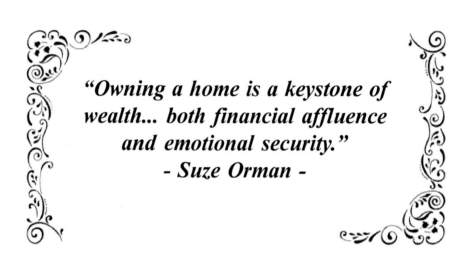

"Owning a home is a keystone of wealth... both financial affluence and emotional security."
- Suze Orman -

Homes

An investment in real estate is likely to be one of the most significant financial decisions you will ever make. A tremendous sense of pride, fulfilment, stability and security comes with owning your own property, particularly your own home.

Increasing property prices and the demand for quality rental accommodation mean that, with a carefully selected and well-managed rental property, landlords can enjoy a return on investment not just from capital appreciation but also from the steady stream of passive income. Even where there are downturns in property values, properties generally continue to rent and often without a corresponding decrease in the rental income. Here are some tips as you consider this investment class.

How will You Finance the Property?

Most people borrow to buy property. Before you buy a property, be sure that you can actually afford it and are able to service and repay the debt. Having a pre-approval in place will save you time and energy as the lender would already have reviewed your financial status to determine how much you can afford and how much they are prepared to lend you. Spending more than you can afford can cause you to default on your mortgage, leading to foreclosure.

Apart from the actual purchase price of a property, which reflects its location, features, age and condition, there are other significant transaction costs that come to bear including lenders fees, valuation and survey fees, estate agents fees, legal fees, transfer taxes, stamp duty and insurance cover. In addition, there are the maintenance and repair costs of holding the asset.

The Importance of Documentation and Title

Whilst the documentation requirements can be cumbersome and can make investing in real estate somewhat tedious, it is important for the security of your investment that all documentation reflecting the true title of the property is in place.

Seek professional advice to determine the most appropriate structure and the vehicle through which you might own the property. There are implications for you and your heirs for holding title in your name, in the name of your beneficiaries as well as in the name of a trust or a limited company.

Location, Location, Location

We have all heard the old adage: "location, location, location." The value of property and the success or failure of this investment is largely dependent upon its location. Neighbourhoods change; market conditions, community issues, the local economic and political environment, poor enforcement of regulatory policies - these can all affect an area adversely and diminish property values considerably.

Risk and Real Estate

Real estate is relatively illiquid and it is risky to invest with a short-term view. Like stock market investing, the property markets go through cycles. Maintain a long-term outlook as it usually takes time, patience and energy to reap the benefits from this investment class.

Unfortunately, the property market, as other financial markets, can be fraught with some unsavoury characters so be very careful with whom you are dealing. Choose your agent carefully; a tested, dependable and responsive professional who comes recommended, has sound market knowledge. Be cautious of high-pressure sales pitches; they can be very persuasive yet a "once in a lifetime opportunity you cannot afford to miss" can turn out to be the worst investment you ever made.

Build Your Knowledge

According to Benjamin Graham, "Investment is most intelligent when it is most businesslike." Do your homework. Every investment comes with a degree of risk and real estate is no different. Rental real estate can provide a steady, long-term income, but it does take some effort to become successful. Indeed, many investors find that things can go horribly wrong.

To be effective as a real estate investor and to obtain the best value for your investments, seek to gain a better understanding of the market so that you can make an educated decision based on research and an assessment of your goals. As far as possible, try to consider an areas current prospects as well as upcoming plans including infrastructural development nearby. By having some knowledge about the specific market one is better equipped to navigate some of the complex nuances of real estate investing and able to predict trends and capture opportunities.

Of course you can never cover all the unknowns and you cannot accurately predict what the property will be worth in a few years, but you can certainly get some sense of its prospects.

Renting Out Your Property

The right tenant can be a joy, but the wrong tenant can make a landlord's life a misery. Some tenants appear to be very pleasant and civilised but you could end up with no rental income and a property in a deplorable state. Request for references and always follow up on them.

Don't Put All Your Eggs In One Basket

As performance in one asset class will help offset any downturn in another as economic and market conditions change over time, it is advisable to spread your risk amongst a range of assets including stocks, bonds and cash rather than concentrating on the property market.

Real estate has long been regarded as a sound and tested investment class that has proven its worth over centuries to be a stable and profitable investment, a trend that long-term investors are likely to continue to enjoy.

I

Insurance

"Too many people ignore the need for insurance until a major mishap or setback occurs; it is then that the impact of inadequate insurance coverage becomes glaring."
- A-Z Of Personal Finance -

I

Insurance

Peter Johnson was a manager in a telecom company. His wife Karen did not work. They had two young children who were enrolled in a private school in the pleasant neighbourhood where the family rented an apartment. They had two nice cars and other luxuries and were able to enjoy a wonderful family holiday abroad at least once a year. The Johnsons were the picture of the perfect family with a bright future. Suddenly, everything changed. Peter, who was 36 years old, had a massive heart attack that killed him instantly.

As morbid as it sounds, can your loved ones afford to lose you? If you were to pass away suddenly, could your family or dependants pay for the funeral, organise the family finances, service any outstanding debt, meet family goals and maintain their current standard of living? Or would they face extreme hardship in the event of the death of their primary breadwinner? The main objective of life insurance is to replace income that would be lost should the policy holder lose his or her life.

We tend to assume that bad things won't happen to us. Too many people ignore the need for insurance until a major mishap or setback occurs; it is then that the impact of inadequate insurance coverage becomes glaring. No matter how meticulous you are with your finances, failure to purchase adequate insurance can impair your financial future and put you or your loved ones in a desperate situation in an instant.

Life, household, health and motor vehicle insurance are just a few of the various policies that are available for consumers. Consider your car, your home and other personal possessions. If these valuables are seriously damaged in an accident or some of your most valuable possessions are stolen, could you afford to replace them? Some types of insurance are compulsory for individuals such as public building insurance and third party cover in respect of motor vehicles. However, for most classes of insurance, it is for you to decide how much cover you should have, given your situation.

Is Your Home Insured?

Can you afford to replace your home? Ideally, your home should be insured for what it would cost to replace or rebuild it if it were destroyed. If you haven't upgraded your home insurance policy in the past few years, you run the risk of having seriously inadequate coverage, as your policy may not have kept up with the rising building or replacement costs.

Do You Have an Educational Policy?

As responsible parents, one of our priorities is to give our children the best start in life, and a sound and qualitative education is one way to do so. As the cost of higher education increases significantly each year, it could put a financial strain on your budget. Many parents thus start planning and preparing for their children's college education in the early years of the children's lives. One method of doing this is to take out an educational plan, which is basically an insurance policy. Various policies are on offer, so closely scrutinise the terms, as having an educational plan may not be enough to cover all the costs when the time comes for your children to enter college but could go some way in offsetting some of the significant costs.

Does Your Family have Medical Insurance in Place?

How healthy are you? If you or anyone in your family were to ever become gravely ill, can you afford the best medical treatment available? If you are generally healthy, it may be a good idea to select a policy with the highest deductible you can afford. A deductible is the part of the expenses that you are required to pay before your insurer covers your health costs. This is to discourage the insured from claiming for the slightest thing. You may pay for routine medical care costs, but will have the peace of mind of knowing that if you become seriously ill, your insurance will kick in.

Insurance offers you cover in return for a monthly, quarterly or annual payment called a premium. It is easy to overlook these payments so don't lose your insurance by neglecting to pay your premiums. It sounds obvious, but you must read your policy carefully to be sure that it provides the cover you need and you must be fully aware of what is excluded.

Whilst insurance will not eliminate the risk of loss or damage to property, injury, illness, or death, it will relieve the insured of some of the financial losses these risks bring. The costs of coverage are far lower than having to service the costs yourself, should the need indeed arise. If you don't have the necessary insurance coverage, do make this one of your financial priorities.

J

Joint Accounts

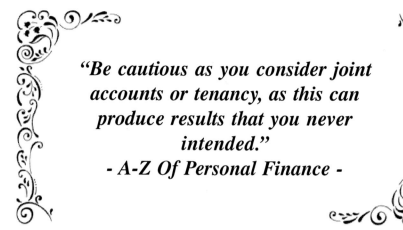

"Be cautious as you consider joint accounts or tenancy, as this can produce results that you never intended."
- A-Z Of Personal Finance -

J

Joint Accounts

Tony grimaced as the cashier handed him back the debit card. "I am sorry sir, but your card has been declined for insufficient funds". Since his marriage to Tina, this has been a problem. Tina was not as responsible with money as he would have liked, as she could be quite frivolous and impulsive about spending. Whatever money was deposited into their joint account through direct debits from their two salary accounts simply evaporated into thin air. Fortunately, Tony always kept some cash on him, so he was able to pay for the groceries.

Tough economic times can strain not only a couple's finances, but their relationship as well; where one partner is less "responsible" with money, the other partner may harbor some resentment. Financial concerns are amongst the most common sources of tension in relationships. Fortunately, planning and communication can help you avoid financial friction and frustrating conversations.

Most people have already established their own financial personality and preferences even before they become part of a couple. For new couples, it pays to start off on the right footing by establishing a fair and open method for dealing with finances; money matters should be discussed and opinions expressed early.

Joint Accounts

Whilst joint accounts are most common amongst married couples, there are other instances and relationships where it may be prudent to operate a joint account. For example, elderly parents may consider opening a joint account with their adult children in order to pay household bills or to avoid the probate court process in the event of their death. Parents may also opt to maintain a joint account with their children in order that they have access to funds should the need arise.

In any partnership there will be shared expenses where, regardless of who actually pays for them, the benefit is shared. These include food, utility bills and larger expenses such as rent or mortgage payments, school fees and family vacations which may be too large for one partner or spouse to handle alone. It is important that there be complete clarity and communication regarding such expenses. If one person earns significantly more or less than the other, it would be fair to contribute amounts in proportion to the respective incomes to reflect this imbalance.

Joint accounts work best where both parties have established a solid level of trust between them. Whilst this offers convenience and transparency, it does mean that each partner becomes financially liable for the other and of course either party can go to the bank and drain the account.

Separate Accounts

If one partner spends money in a way that the other considers frivolous, or if one partner finds a joint account restrictive, as it affords less privacy and independence, it is probably best to have separate accounts.

Being able to spend money without having your partner scrutinise the minutest detail is certainly important to some.

Even though there may be no need to question each other's personal expenses such as clothing, personal luxuries and hobbies, it is advisable that both parties still be involved and consulted about significant financial decisions. There must be a conscious effort to keep the greater financial picture in mind, as with separate finances one may lose sight of the family's long-term goals.

Joint and Separate Accounts

Having a joint account for certain large and recurring expenses combined with individual accounts for personal expenses is a good compromise. Particular expenses may be assigned where one party pays for certain bills whilst the other partner pays for others. This is probably the most popular system, where each partner takes some responsibility for maintaining the household budget yet each still retains some independence.

As the global economic crunch continues to bite, family partnerships the world over are affected, with many experiencing financial concerns for the first time in their relationship. Today, most households or families require two incomes in order to sustain a comfortable standard of living and lifestyle and to build a secure financial future.

There is no one size fits all; some couples have joint accounts, whilst others prefer to keep their finances separate. Even the best system is not always appropriate for every circumstance, so plan to modify your system as your relationship and financial situation evolves. If one system doesn't work, just try a different one. Regardless of which option you choose, it is important that both parties discuss money matters.

K

Kids

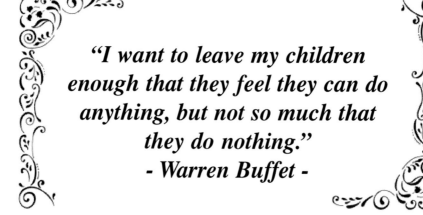

"I want to leave my children enough that they feel they can do anything, but not so much that they do nothing."
- Warren Buffet -

Kids

Parents are often faced with a dilemma; we want our children to have better lives and opportunities than we ever had and want to give them the best of everything. Driven by a natural instinct to love, nurture and provide for them, we run the risk of overindulging or spoiling our children, which can have dire consequences for their future, as it may prevent them from reaching their full potential.

When children are deprived of the opportunity to be self reliant, they develop a sense of entitlement that shields them from the desire to work hard. Overindulgence can lead to a loss of motivation, which comes from having every whim satisfied and never having to take care of basic needs for themselves. This could leave them ill-equipped to cope with the real world and financially dependent on parents who should be catering to their retirement. On the more sinister side, they can become financially irresponsible, and out of desperation, be tempted to maintain a certain lifestyle at all costs.

The elementary school years, when children are being introduced to mathematics concepts and coming to grips with numbers, are an excellent time to lay a solid foundation in personal financial management. Sadly, our educational system focuses almost totally on academic subjects, and rarely is any aspect of money management taught in schools.

If we want our children to grow up to be financially responsible adults, we must introduce them to the fundamentals of personal finance from an early age; they should have some basic understanding and practical experience in spending, saving, banking and investing. This will help them to develop a responsible attitude towards money and provide them with sufficient grounding for making sensible financial decisions in future.

Teach them to Save

One of the simplest ways to encourage a responsible attitude about money is to encourage children to save. Little children get excited about their "piggybank"; this traditional first savings method helps to build initial interest. Today some piggybanks have various compartments for saving, spending, investing and giving; the children can then decide where their money goes.

Naturally, as children get older, and begin to save more deliberately, it is important that you visit a bank with them to make a deposit into an account opened in their name to reinforce what you are teaching at home. Many banks offer incentives and attractive savings account options tailored for children. Explain the concept of earning interest on their savings. Saving towards goals encourages a sense of motivation. Encourage them to keep a record of how they are saving and spending their money; this will set the stage for budgeting. An ATM card may be introduced when they are eligible.

Saving Towards Goals

Teaching children to set specific, measurable goals encourages a sense of motivation. Very young children tend to lose interest in goals that take too long to achieve. For them, set modest, attainable savings goals. Over time, your children will learn to become more disciplined savers and can save for longer-term goals for large-ticket items like a camera or a computer. Offering to match whatever your children save towards a long-term goal can be an incentive to older children and spur them onto attaining a goal.

Write down each goal and the amount that must be saved weekly, or monthly to reach it. This will help your children learn the difference between short-term and long-term goals and how best to save or invest to achieve them.

Teach them to Budget

Learning how to live within ones means is an important aspect of daily life, and creating a budget is one of the best ways to achieve this. Sit down with your children and go over their wants and needs. What are they saving towards? How much can they afford? What items or gifts do they plan to buy? Include some of their bills into their monthly budget such as the cost of maintaining their mobile phone.

Take them to the market or grocery store, and explain how you compare items based on price and quality. Talk about the purchases of the day, the way you select and get value for money. Through commercials and peer pressure, children are constantly tempted to make impulsive purchases and will need guidance from you about how to make sound buying decisions.

Give them an Allowance

A regular allowance or "pocket money" is often a child's first experience with financial independence, as it gives them a certain degree of control over their own money and provides an effective learning opportunity in earning, budgeting, saving and prioritising purchases. Children should have some money of their own so they can learn how to manage it.

In deciding on the amount for an allowance, it is important to consider what items the money should cover be based on their age and what your family can afford. It should be enough for the children to be able to pay for their basic wants and still have a little left over for saving. Naturally, children should not have access to excessive sums of money. Some parents give a "bonus" for good performance at school. Be cautious if you choose to reward them monetarily, as this could prevent them from developing a keen sense of responsibility for themselves.

Guide and advise, but don't dictate how the money should be saved or spent. Whilst an allowance does require some supervision - and you do need to set some parameters around the types of purchases you expect them to make - as far as possible, avoid micromanaging and querying every expense. Allow them to determine their own spending choices whilst encouraging them to keep a record of how they are saving and spending their money, thus setting the stage for budgeting.

Learning to Earn

Some parents pay their children for doing chores around the house, whilst others prefer to give an allowance with no strings attached. Chores offer an important lesson in cooperation and develop a sense of responsibility in children as they live within their family community. Try not to tie chores too stringently to allowances, as this can make children feel that being paid for helping out at home is their right rather than their duty. Some parents soon find themselves having to negotiate to get anything done! You do not want them developing the idea that they must be paid for everything they do. However, it makes sense to allow them to earn extra money for tasks that fall outside the usual household responsibilities, and they benefit immensely from learning to earn.

Encourage your teenagers to earn. Children tend to be much more disciplined and careful with money that they worked hard for than with their "free" pocket money or allowance. When the money comes out of their own pocket they tend to be more selective and sensitive about their purchases. A part-time or vacation job is ideal for developing a work ethic and often provides teenagers with their first earnings.

Once young adults graduate and start earning their own income, they should be encouraged to contribute towards some of the household expenses, even where you do not need the supplementary income. If they live totally expense free, they may not see the need to save or budget.

Teach them to Give

Instead of giving them too much, encourage your children to give of themselves to others. You can provide opportunities for them to be caring, giving and sensitive human beings. Involve your children in your financial decisions regarding philanthropy and expose them to charitable giving early in their lives. Children can donate their outgrown toys, books and clothes and as they get older, can volunteer of their time and talent.

These lessons teach them to understand and value those less fortunate than themselves and will go a long way in creating a more responsible, caring society as the younger generation begins to develop a sense of appreciation for some of the experiences and luxuries that they enjoy and often take forgranted. By encouraging this early in their lives, children become more empathic adults who can make a positive impact on the community in which they live.

Be a Good Role Model

Action speaks louder than words. Your children will learn about money values primarily through your behaviour; they learn from what they see, hear and experience. If you set a good example and demonstrate the importance of hard work, it will have a positive impact on them. On the other hand, if your lifestyle displays ostentatious, obscene extravagance, this will become the example that they come to live by and could impact on your children in more ways than you can imagine. The way you deal with money issues, from settling bills to making a large, affordable purchases, are all-important lessons that will remain with them.

Bringing up children to develop a healthy attitude towards money as they grow from childhood to adulthood is a challenging yet rewarding process that requires some commitment and consistency. The life-long benefit this brings makes it well worth the effort. Even if you can afford to fund everything that your children want, try to restrain yourself and teach them to learn to distinguish between wants and needs. This will not only help the family finances in challenging times but will also prepare them to lead disciplined lives.

Too many of us look back on life and wish that we had started investing when we were young. Begin early in your children's lives to instill in them the important building blocks of saving and investing and start them off in the right direction towards a secure financial future.

———————————————————

L

Long-Term

"*In the long run, a portfolio of well-chosen stocks and/or equity mutual funds will always outperform a portfolio of bonds or a money-market account. In the long run, a portfolio of poorly chosen stocks won't outperform the money left under the mattress.*"
- *Peter Lynch* -

Long-Term

A year ago, Benson's investment in a stock mutual fund was valued at $120,000. Today it has lost more than half of its value and is worth only $58,000. He is devastated and fearful that the situation may get even worse. The money was set aside specifically to pay for his master's degree in a program scheduled for September. His dilemma is: should he go ahead and cash out of this faltering investment and place the funds in a short-term money market account or should she leave the money where it is in the hope that the market will correct itself by August, when he must pay his school fees?

The hard truth is that Benson's money should never have been invested in the stock market in the first place, but should have been saved in money market instruments. Unless he has an alternative source of funds, Benson may have to sell enough of his stock investments to pay his school fees or may be forced to defer his plans. As anyone who has invested in stocks has experienced, when you do not have time on your side, stock market investing comes with significant risk.

What does Long Term Really Mean?

One of the best pieces of investment advice ever given by financial advisors is to look at investing as a long-term activity both in bear markets when prices are falling as well as in bull markets where stock prices are going up. Yet people in the financial world are often accused of never really clarifying exactly what "long-term" means except to say that cash required for immediate needs should not be invested in the stock market. Beyond that, a long investment horizon could mean three to five years and much longer.

Spread Your Risk and be Diversified

Whether you have invested for the short-term or the long-term, make sure you have managed your risk with a diversified, well-balanced portfolio. Most investments do not reach their full potential for several years. Usually, within that length of time, long-term investors, especially those who invest in a diversified portfolio, can ride out market volatility without dramatically affecting their ability to reach their goals. It is important to seek financial advice so that a financial plan can be designed to achieve your unique financial goals.

Keep Investing

In bear markets many investors tend to panic and bail out of poorly performing investments. By doing this, they crystallise their losses and let go of some assets that are likely to recover once the markets rebound. Don't let your emotions get the better of you and derail your overall investment plan. By sticking with your long-term investment strategy during a bear market you are putting yourself in the best position to profit in a bull market when the market begins to turnaround.

Whether you have investing for the short-term or the long-term, make sure you have managed your risk with a diversified, well-balanced portfolio so that you can ride out market volatility without dramatically affecting your ability to reach your goals. It is important to seek financial advice so that a financial plan can be designed to achieve your unique financial goals and circumstances.

No one can tell for how long a bear market will last. The biggest mistake you can make is to stop investing for your long-term goals. If you are paralysed with fear from past experience, or move all your funds into the money market, it will be harder for your portfolio to recover when the markets rally, and they will.

Cost averaging is a strategy often recommended by financial advisors for investors to set aside a certain amount on a regular basis. Using this approach, an investor buys fewer shares when prices are high and more when they are low thus reducing the overall average cost. Naturally this has strong appeal for investors who are still scarred by a stock market crash and are wary of placing a large sum into the market all at once.

Stocks are ideal long-term investments; very few people have made enduring fortunes overnight in the stock market; those that have truly built wealth in the markets have been patient and have had a long-term view. History is the best teacher; though you won't be able to avoid temporary losses during a downturn, the long-term has been much kinder to investments. Don't let your patience run out, or your emotions get the better of you. Stay the course, take advantage of opportunities and think long-term.

M

Marriage

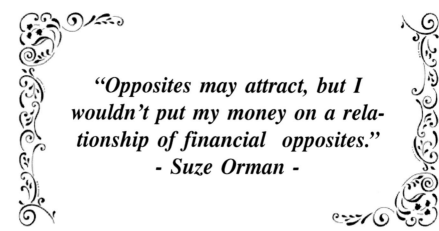

"Opposites may attract, but I wouldn't put my money on a relationship of financial opposites."
- Suze Orman -

Marriage

Even the best system may not always be appropriate so be prepared to adjust as your relationship and financial situation evolve.

About Love and Money

When two people become a couple they confront a myriad of financial choices and decisions. If you are engaged, how much do you know about your fiance's financial situation? After the excitement of the wedding ceremonies, it will be time to face your financial future together. Research shows that financial concerns are one of the most common sources of tension in a relationship and have some part in most divorces. Most couples nevertheless go into marriage without ever broaching the subject of finances. It may not be romantic, but it is important. Here are some of the money issues that you should discuss with your future spouse or partner.

What is Your Attitude About Money?

You do not just develop good or bad money habits by chance; attitudes about money are formed very early in life and usually develop over many years. You may not even realise the full effect of your childhood experiences, circumstances and your parents' attitudes about money; indeed many people simply assume the savings and money management habits of their parents. Were they very frugal, disciplined savers, or were they spendthrifts? The way you view money can have a significant impact on the financial decisions you make.

Talk About Money

Talking about money can be a little awkward in the early stages of a relationship. Most couples have different attitudes about money, which are formed long before we meet our partners. Such experiences can influence your spending, saving and investing habits, need for security, ability to bear risk, attitudes about debt and so on.

What are Your Financial Goals?

What are your short- medium- and long-term goals? Where do you see yourselves five, ten and twenty years from now? Financially this can mean owning your own home, educating your children and planning for your retirement.

In relationships there may be different goals and priorities. One partner may be averse to debt; for the other debt is a way of life. He might want a flashy car, whilst she might feel more secure with money in the bank. She might spend all the housekeeping money on jewelry, shoes and bags, whilst his priority is to give the children a sound education. He may view the new home cinema as their greatest new asset, whilst her priority is to make a down payment on a new home. If the differences are fundamental, this will be a source of conflict. At the same time, be conscious of the fact that it shouldn't be all about scrimping and saving towards the future; treat yourselves sometimes.

How do You Feel about Budgeting?

It is surprising how many married couples get by without a budget. Through budgeting you have a better idea of what is coming in and how much is going out. You should both know how much you pay for your rent or mortgage, utility bills, insurance and so on. Budgeting responsibilities should be shared so that neither partner feel the need to shoulder all the responsibility. Periodic meetings, say once a month, are useful to review bank balances, any outstanding debt, routine expenses, as well as any major expenses that need careful planning.

How Much Debt are you Bringing to the Marriage?

Many people do not discover the full extent of their spouse's financial obligations until they are married. Debt brought into marriage can be a major source of strife if not well handled. Each partner should know the debt load the other one carries, as once you are married that debt load is usually shared. Whilst you are not legally responsible for the loans opened in your partner's name, it could certainly affect your eligibility for joint loans such as a mortgage. It should be a priority to try to deal with it together and bring it under control.

Who Pays for What?

Something as basic as the handling of everyday household expenses is a source of friction in many families. How will you handle routine household expenses? You both earn, but how much should each person contribute? Are you both doing your "share?" Should it be equal amounts or a certain percentage no matter what each person earns? If one of you earns significantly more or less than the other, it seems only fair to contribute amounts in proportion to your respective incomes to reflect this imbalance.

Some couples assign specific expenses; you pay the rent and school fees, and i'll pay for groceries, utilities and so on. Other couples use one partner's income for all expenses and apply the other's income to building up their savings and investments.

Who will Manage the Family Finances?

Women often enter marriage assuming that their spouse will handle all money issues, thus delegating almost total financial responsibility and sitting on the sidelines without being involved. Determine which of you is best able to manage routine, everyday financial matters. Teamwork is essential, and shared duties work well for some families but even if one party is more involved, both should have a general overview of the total picture. Periodic meetings are important so you both know where you stand financially and can see whether you are actually moving closer towards your family goals.

Should You have Separate or Joint Accounts or a Combination of the Two?

Should you open a joint account and pool both incomes or have separate accounts? Having a joint account combined with individual accounts for personal expenses is a good compromise, as each partner takes some responsibility for the household budget yet is still able to retain some autonomy. Partners can contribute a certain amount of their monthly salary into the joint account to cover routine household expenses such as food, utilities and so on. Some couples decide to put their salaries into the joint account and then give themselves a monthly allowance.

Remember that parties to a joint account have a right to withdraw all the money in that account. It is for this reason that the use of a joint account is usually limited to couples that have built a solid level of trust between themselves. Look critically at the options, and try to accommodate one another.

Should You Set Spending Limits?

Do you have to account for everything you spend to your spouse or partner? If you show up with an expensive new TV or a car, could this be a cause of tension? Everyone needs some personal spending money that doesn't have to be accounted for. The amount will vary depending on the couple's resources and lifestyle. Some couples set spending limits on how much either party can spend without consulting each other.

Tough economic times can cause a strain not only a couple's finances, but indeed on their relationship. However, even though there may be the occasional conflict about money, it is really about how best these conflicts are resolved. With careful planning, clear communication and compromise, you can avoid many frustrating conversations.

There is no one size fits all when it comes to finances in relationships. Even the best approach may not always be appropriate so be prepared to adjust as your relationship and financial situation evolve. Try to find the right balance that works for your situation; if one option doesn't work, try another. The financial decisions that you make now can have a lasting impact on your financial future as you embark on life's journey together.

M

Mutual Funds

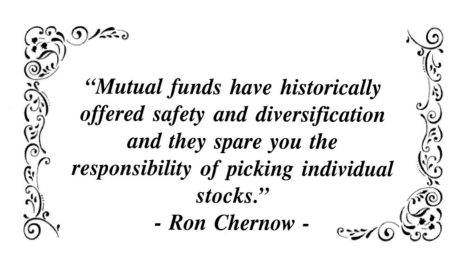

"Mutual funds have historically offered safety and diversification and they spare you the responsibility of picking individual stocks."
- Ron Chernow -

Mutual Funds

Have you been thinking about investing in stocks but aren't quite sure how to start? Perhaps you don't have the time or know how to select your own stocks or do not have a very large amount of money to invest. Mutual Funds may be the ideal investment option for you.

A Mutual Fund is a portfolio that pools investor's funds to purchase stocks, bonds, money market and other securities. When you invest in a mutual fund, you own a piece of the total portfolio of securities. The portfolio is then managed by a professional fund manager who handles everything from the day to day management of the fund including research, selection and monitoring of the performance of the fund and its underlying investments.

There are several different mutual funds to choose from. Some invest purely in stocks, some in bonds, whilst others invest in short-term money market securities; balanced funds invest in combinations of these categories.

Whether your goal is to give your children an excellent education, to give yourself a secure, comfortable retirement, to buy a new home or to travel the world, mutual funds can help you to achieve your goals. Carefully consider your goals, your risk tolerance, your time horizon and your financial situation in determining the mutual fund that will best meet your needs.

Mutual funds usually set relatively low minimum amounts for initial and subsequent subscriptions. This makes it an idea investment product for smaller investors who do not have a lump sum to invest but prefer to set aside funds periodically for long-term savings.

Consider a simple cost averaging strategy of systematically investing a fixed sum periodically say monthly or quarterly in a mutual fund. This is a particularly useful method in a volatile market as you can reduce the average cost of your shares by purchasing more shares when prices are low and fewer shares when they are high. A consistent disciplined approach takes away the speculative element of investing and reduces stress and fear.

Investing without proper knowledge is one of the worst investment mistakes. Every mutual fund publishes a prospectus which is a legal document that provides a great deal of information that you need to know and understand, such as the fund's investment objective and style and its fees. Always review a fund's prospectus before committing your funds. Most mutual funds provide online access, which makes it easy for you to monitor your investment. Fund bid and offer prices are also quoted in the dailies.

Mutual fund investments are very liquid and you can easily sell or redeem your shares in an open-ended fund at any time; it will usually take a week to receive payment. It is important to note that you can lose money in a mutual fund. With the exception of money market funds, prices of mutual funds will fluctuate. However, the longer you leave your money invested, the greater the success you are likely to have.

Mutual funds are not insured or guaranteed by any government agency, however the Securities and Exchange Commission has oversight over the capital market and mutual fund companies must operate under strict guidelines.

One of the most valued and lasting gifts a parent can give a child is the knowledge of investing, and mutual funds are an ideal place to start. Children have the benefit of time, so are in a good position to take advantage of investments which can be left to appreciate in value over several years. Whilst a minor cannot open a mutual fund account, an adult can hold units of the fund on their behalf.

Do remember that any money that you place in the stock market must be seen as a long-term investment. Funds that you need to set aside for your rent should have been placed in a short-term money market account. If you do not have any other easily accessible funds, you may be forced to sell your shares at a loss to secure your accommodation.

It is important to spread your investments over different asset classes, so that a loss in a particular investment may be minimised by gains in another. Mutual funds offer diversification and help you spread your risk.

No one can predict what the financial markets will do in the next few days, weeks, months or years. Volatility is a necessary fact of investing. During a bull market greed drives stock prices up; this attracts even more people to the party. On the other hand, investors tend to be fearful during bear markets. Fear creates panic selling, which forces prices downward regardless of a company's prospects. This presents a buying opportunity as ultimately, that long-term economic value will eventually pull the stock price back up in line with its fundamental realities.

In spite of the fact that the stock market will inevitably go through periods of turbulence, the superior returns of a carefully executed long-term investment strategy can generally outweigh the risks involved.

N

Networth vs Selfworth

"As materialism becomes endemic and a society equates selfworth with networth with far too much emphasis placed on money, power, position and possessions, and acknowledges and celebrates wealth without questioning its source, there is a tendency for people to go to extremes in order to increase their networth at all costs and by any means possible leading to dishonesty and corruption."
- A-Z Of Personal Finance -

Networth versus Selfworth

Networth is an external measure of how much we are worth in financial terms, while selfworth is an internal measure of how much one values oneself. In our society, there is a tendency to attach selfworth and other people's approval to material things and shows of ostentation.

The Dangers of Materialism

A society that celebrates a person's worth based on his or her assets, connections and influence is materialistic as it builds a social strata based on material things. When people are "encouraged" to amass and cling to possessions, when our pursuit is on making profit, pursuing pleasure, and obtaining position, it leaves little energy, time and ability to focus on our real purpose and the things that really matter.

A materialistic society rates individuals not on personal character and achievement, but rather on the fantastic display that they are able to put on in the form of and other extreme shows of ostentation. Where a societal value system has evolved in which material fortune is more widely celebrated than diligence, honesty, honour and integrity; these virtues are seldom accorded the respect they do deserve.

As materialism becomes endemic and a society equates self-worth with networth with far too much emphasis placed on money, power, position and possessions, and acknowledges and celebrates wealth without questioning its source, there is a tendency for people to go to extremes in order to increase their networth at all costs and by any means possible leading to dishonesty and corruption.

As people compete to build the trappings of wealth and put these on display, the seeds of corruption are sown. Greed and the insatiable love for materialism are at the root of bribery and corruption, which have eaten deep into the marrow of our society. The endless desire of all strata of society, both rich and poor, for possessions, inevitably leads to moral decadence.

How do You Measure Yourself?

Have you ever thought of how you measure yourself? Reflect on whether you have measured yourself through your job, your money, your position, or your possessions. Does your selfworth come from your job and all its perks, your money, your position in government or in the private sector and the attendant trappings, or your position in society?

The Next Generation

Children often identify their selfworth with the approval of their peers, which could be linked to how many toys they have, or how expensive their clothes are, or how quickly they acquire the latest blackberry, iPhone, iPad or other gadget.

Stories abound of children asking to be dropped off before the school gate so that their peers won't see the car they arrived in. If it is not an expensive car or jeep, it could be embarrassing as they face jeers. In an excerpt from *The Vanishing Adolescent* 1959, Edgar Z. Friedenberg writes, "What we must decide is perhaps how we are valuable rather than how valuable we are".

To release the next generation from the scourge of materialism, we must teach our children to be proud of whom they are, to value themselves and not to confuse their selfworth with their networth. Parents and leaders must teach their children and our youth, by example, that their true value lies in their inner qualities — their kindness, sensitivity, creativity, compassion, rather than their looks, performance, possessions and how much money their parents may or may not have. They must be taught to embrace hard work and diligence as a means to success and not be under peer pressure to look for shortcuts to "get rich quick".

Why is Selfworth Important?

Life is not about accumulating wealth and possessions, because in the end, you cannot take them away with you. We often feel a false sense of security by having a large networth or more wealth than our neighbour. As we have seen in the recent past, networth and fortunes can change dramatically; wealth can be transient and all can change in an instant. During periods of economic turmoil and stockmarket declines, investors have lost fortunes; properties worth billions will be worth only a tiny percentage of their "value" if there are no buyers. Wealth is nice to have and can and does bring pleasure but it is important to keep it in perspective. A strong sense of selfworth is the key to true and lasting fulfillment.

Primary success of which selfworth is a part and includes character, integrity, humility, service above self and legacy are far more important than secondary success of networth that is associated with title, position, bank accounts, properties and cars.

In their study "Inner Security and Infinite Wealth: Merging Self-Worth and NetWorth", Stuart Zimmerman and Jared Rosen contrast the idea of networth, an external measure of how much money one may or may not have, and selfworth, an internal appraisal of one's own worth. They suggest that in order to develop a sense of well being beyond material success and its outward trappings, we should strive to become more aware of what is truly important in life and what legacy we will leave behind.

Calculating Your Networth

Your networth is a snapshot of what you own, your assets, less the debt that you owe; your liabilities. Your networth gives you a true picture of what you *actually* own and is one of the most accurate measures of your financial progress. It can be a useful tool with which to track your progress year on year.

Calculating your networth is a fairly straightforward process. Before you embark on this exercise, get yourself organised and gather all your financial documentation; your bank statements, investment advices, receipts and so on. Here are some simple steps to help you to calculate your networth.

- List your major assets: Get a realistic value of your car, your home and any other property you might own. It is best to be conservative in your estimates so that you do not distort the true picture of your networth. Particularly during a major recession, real estate is not easily marketable so you must be realistic in your estimates.
- List other assets such as cash, bank accounts, certificates of deposit, stocks, bonds, mutual funds, retirement savings and life insurance policies that have accumulated cash value.
- Do you have any valuable personal effects such as jewelry, an expensive wristwatch, a musical instrument, some special furniture or valuable artwork, a serious coin or stamp collection or any family heirlooms? Don't list everything, just things of significant value. Be sure to list the *market* value of your assets

as their *real* value is only what the market is prepared to pay for them and not what you would like the value to be.

- Add all the assets that you have listed to get your total asset figure. This information is also very useful in ensuring that you have adequate insurance coverage.
- Now list your personal liabilities or what you owe such as your mortgage, car loan, outstanding debt on your credit cards and any other debt.
- Add up all your liabilities to come up with a total.
- Subtract this total from your total assets and there you will have your networth. A negative figure should jolt you into making necessary changes in your financial situation.
- Try to go through this process at least once a year and track your progress. Ideally, you should have a steadily increasing networth.

N

Next of Kin

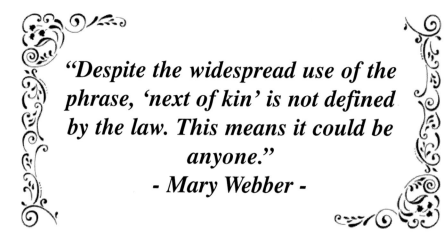

"Despite the widespread use of the phrase, 'next of kin' is not defined by the law. This means it could be anyone."
- Mary Webber -

N

Next of Kin

Who is Your Next of Kin?

There are several factors that people consider in choosing their next of kin. Here are some responses to the question "Who is your Next of Kin?"

Florence Dottie: A Businesswoman (Married)

I chose my husband as my next of kin because he should be the first person to know whatever happens to me. The meaning of next of kin is someone that can be reached quickly in case of any emergencies or issues and that person to me is my husband. And he is the closest person to me.

Oscar: A Businessman (Single)

My younger sister is my next of kin. I chose her because we are very close, and I think she is the only person I can trust for now, as I am not married. All my documents, such as my life insurance policy and bank details, have her down as my next of kin although she is not aware of this.

Mrs Sobo: A Banker (Married)

My first son is my next of kin because he is the heir. If I choose my daughters, they will get married one day and their husbands could take over all that they have, and family property will then end up in a strange family. My son is a man, he controls the home and no woman would dare take over what is rightfully his. I can never choose my husband; that's how he will go and marry again, and the woman will use all my property to benefit her own children and neglect mine.

Charles: A Trader

I will put my brother. I know him well - we grew up together. I wouldn't make my wife my next of kin, though I love her so much. If I put one of her children, she will influence them. Women can change. It is better to be safe than sorry.

Mrs Campbell: A Teacher

My daughters are my next of kin. If you notice, female children always look after their parents in old age. Your daughter will never abandon you even if she marries and lives far away. Woe betide you if your son marries a wicked woman. You are finished!

Mr Johnson: A Taxi Driver

Ah! I will put my first son. I expect him to take care of all the family if I am not there. I can never put my wife - that's how she will go and marry, and then some other man will be enjoying all my sweat and blood. Just the thought that she might be enjoying my money with another man after my death puts me off. Ah, no-oh! Never!

Mrs Smith: A Lawyer

It depends. I can put my husband down but I have to watch him closely for some years. I will look at how he behaves. If I see that he is unfaithful, and I can no longer trust him, I will take him off and put my sister.

Mr Kenneth: A Teacher

I have already put my father – he is very wise and can only do what is right for me. He will make sure my wife and children do not suffer.

Maribel: A Trader (Married)

My husband is my next of kin. We love and trust each other and are building everything together. He was there before any children came, so whatever affects me will affect him. I am sure he too will choose me as his next of kin.

The word kin in the traditional sense means family, which apart from a spouse and children goes on to include the extended family, parents, siblings, cousins, uncles, aunts and so on. The term "next-of-kin" is rather ambiguous and is usually used to describe a person's closest living blood relative. In its broadest sense it indicates the person who should be notified in case of any eventualities of life such as an accident, emergency, or death. It also has implications as to who would be legally entitled to a decedents property where there is no will.

At some time or the other, you have probably had to fill out a form or some other documentation where you had to clearly state your next of kin. Many people don't take this designation that seriously and sometimes even forget whom they designated as time goes by. This is an important issue particularly where the documentation you are completing relates to money matters such as investments in stocks, real estate, banking and insurance transactions and so on.

If you were to die intestate, that is, without leaving a will, your property won't simply pass to your spouse as you might think; strict rules rank your next of kin, and your property will be distributed according to laws of intestacy, which may vary from state to state.

If there is no will or other credible document in place, this is likely to be the order: If you are married, it would be your spouse. If you are a single parent or are widowed, your children will be your next of kin. If you are unmarried and without children, your parents will be legal heirs to your estate; if your parents are deceased your property will be distributed to siblings and other close blood relatives.

In Western cultures, the choice of the spouse as next of kin is the most obvious one, for example, the mother of his children is generally the person in whom a man places the most trust. In Nigeria, for example, it is more common for a man to choose his brother as next of kin. In the event of the husband's death making the wife your next of kin will save her and the children a lot of hardship given the traditional extended family system where other family members often forcefully claim their brother's property. There are numerous examples there of widows having to cope with not only the loss of their spouse but also of all their personal possessions and property.

Bear in mind that the status of next of kin does not in any way imply that those designated stand to inherit any of the individual's estate in the event of their death. A will is just one tool that can protect your immediate family, including your wife and children, and ensure that your investments and property do not go into the wrong hands after your death.

O

Old Age

"In today's world is it unrealistic to assume that your adult children will take care of you when you are old? What makes the best sense is to start planning early to make provision for that phase of your life after active retirement, so that you are prepared for it whether or not they are able to provide the required support."
- A-Z Of Personal Finance -

O

Old Age

With the lack of a formal, comprehensive and effective social security system, the diminishing role of families in old age care leaves a huge void.

Will Your Children Take Care of You When You are Old?

Many families consist of not only the nuclear family, which is made up of parents and their children, but of the extended family, which embraces several generations of people who are related by blood, marriage, or adoption. In Nigeria, for example, the family is the very foundation of a nations social fabric and includes siblings, grandparents, aunts, uncles, cousins and even more distant relatives.

The Unwritten Rule

The extended family system (EFS) has evolved into a homegrown version of a more formal welfare system. Traditionally, the elderly have been revered and adored and after all their sacrifice they do deserve rest and comfort in old age. Care of the elderly in our midst is culturally rooted and is part of a nation's core values. It has indeed become a shining example of social security within communities.

Through this basic economic unit, family members - typically adult children - are usually charged with the responsibility for the provision of informal care and support for the elderly. Such care and support are generally voluntary and reciprocal and seen as a duty that has been assumed and embraced and that comes without any form of formal compensation.

The unwritten rule is that one's children will play an important role in providing economic security and care for aged parents and in turn, these parents once they become old, should be able to rely on their children.

The Changing Structure of the Family

More recently, there has been a gradual but noticeable shift away from the traditional family towards the nuclear family at the expense of the wider family network and particularly of the elderly, for whom this social phenomenon has served as a form of insurance. It was the traditional economic safety net for old age.

The traditional role of families in caring for their elderly is gradually diminishing due to economic realities that have hindered the willingness and indeed the ability for family members to give. That sense of duty is being overtaken by the daily challenges that family members face in taking care of their own most basic needs. Rural-urban migration, modernisation and influences from foreign cultures are also leading to the gradual disintegration of our communal sense of living. According to a study by sociologists, the past ten years have seen a 70 percent increase in Indian households with nuclear families; this community, like African communities, has traditionally maintained a communal existence.

Rural-Urban Migration

With more than half of the world's population moving towards towns and cities, there is a trend towards urbanisation. Advances in careers often require mobility, which usually means migrating from family in search of employment. The elderly thus remain in their hometowns without adequate care and attention.

Homes for the Elderly

Whilst the concept of senior citizens' homes seems almost alien in African culture, such practical steps must be encouraged where there is no alternative and families are unable to provide even the most basic care for their elderly. Currently there are very few homes that provide for the destitute, elderly or those without family or savings, or for those too frail to work.

Ageing as a Policy Issue

With the lack of a formal comprehensive and effective social security system, and with fledgling pensions and healthcare insurance market schemes in many developing countries, the diminishing role of families involved in care for the elderly leaves a huge void. There is thus an urgent need to refocus on the issues of ageing in Africa and elsewhere. Ageing has become a global phenomenon and indeed a critical policy issue with serious implications. With shifts from the traditional issues of high mortality and high fertility, to reduced fertility and greater longevity, developing countries face an ageing crisis.

The private sector should also begin to direct its philanthropy to include provision for the elderly. Non-governmental organisations and religious organisations such as the Senior Citizens Care Foundation, the African Gerontological Society (AGES) and the Catholic Church, among others, have made laudable efforts in providing assistance to older people through daycare centers, residential homes and regular medical check-ups.

Planning for Your Old Age

In today's world is it unrealistic to assume that your adult children will take care of you when you are old? What makes the best sense is to start planning early to make provision for that phase of your life after active retirement, so that you are prepared for it whether or not they are able to provide the required support. Without adequate planning for retirement, with family resources stretched to the limit, and confronted by increasingly expensive healthcare, many people could face a grim old age.

Financial security is a factor in successful aging and will help the elderly maintain dignity, independence and autonomy beyond the active retirement years. The main contribution made by a balanced portfolio consisting of shares, bonds, cash and real estate, is in providing access to a decent standard of living and in being able to afford long-term healthcare where it is not readily available within the family.

Nowadays, there appears to be a dwindling regard for our elderly. A nation in which the elderly are neglected and even abandoned is reprehensible. It is thus important for all of us to take individual responsibility looking after and protecting the elderly in our midst.

Until an organised and effective welfare and social security system is in place, it is expected that the extended family system will continue to play a crucial role in the social welfare of its members. At the same time, it is clear that as cultural values, socioeconomic conditions and technology continue to evolve so too will the face and structure of the extended family in our contemporary society. In whatever form it takes, it is our responsibility to protect it.

P

Passive Income

"My rich dad taught me to focus on passive income and spend my time acquiring the assets that provide passive or long term residual income…passive income from capital gains, dividends, residual incomefrom business, rental income from real estate, and royalties."

- Robert Kiyosaki -

P

Passive Income

Make Your Money Work for You

Charles often wondered how his colleague Benneth - who was on the same job level, with the same salary, and who had similar skills and experience - could afford to move to a better area, buy a decent car, and even take his family on holiday abroad whilst he (Charles) was still struggling to survive from month to month. Benneth was smart about using some of his salary to generate supplementary income. He has been saving since he started earning and, with the extra income he generated, is well on his way towards achieving financial independence and securing his family's financial future.

What is Passive Income?

The salary you get from work comes as a direct result of your efforts at work. Passive income, on the other hand, generally includes income that is not directly related to your daily activity, income that you can generate without having to actively work for it; in fact, it is the other way round; your money is actually working for you with no extra effort on your part other than the act of investing.

Passive Income in Retirement

If you are middle aged, your goal should be to use as much of your income as possible from your remaining peak-earning years to create a source of passive income, which is often the only source of funds for most people during retirement. It is particularly important to create sources of passive income that will generate regular income for you during retirement or should you be unable to work for a period of time.

Common Sources of Passive Income:

Buy to Let

You can buy residential or commercial property for investment purposes and rent it out to create rental income. For example, in Nigeria where rental income is often earned two to three years in advance, landlords have a huge opportunity to invest the windfall payment derived from one property to invest in another. This can be a great investment for the long-term but usually requires significant capital.

Dividend-Yielding Stocks

One of the easiest ways to earn passive income is to buy shares in a publicly quoted company – one whose shares are listed on the official Stock Exchange - that regularly pays dividends to its shareholders. If you don't have the time or the inclination to carefully select stocks yourself, contact a reputable stock broker and educate yourself on the workings of the stock market. There is a plethora of information online, in books, magazines and the media on how to invest in stocks. As an alternative you might prefer to purchase mutual funds as a good way to build a well diversified and professionally managed portfolio even if you don't have enough money to buy individual stocks.

Both stocks and real estate have the ability to grow in value over time. Indeed, capital appreciation is one of the greatest benefits of both of these passive income sources when you sell your assets. These proceeds can then be used to create other assets.

In discussing the advantages of investing in these sources of passive income, one should never ignore the ensuing risk. Bear in mind that there is the very real risk of loss, as markets can be volatile and prices can fluctuate.

Interest Income

Interest is a most basic form of passive income. This recurring income stream can help finance some of your current needs or be saved for other goals. Interest earned on your savings account balance, fixed deposits, or bonds is a risk-free source of passive income. However, do note that with current interest rates barely keeping apace with inflation, it will be difficult for you to increase your capital in this way.

Invest in a Business

There are many interesting business ventures that struggle and fail to attract adequate funding. If you are approached by a well-regarded entrepreneur to lend money or to invest in his or her business, and are interested in providing some support, have the proposal properly analyzed by a professional before you consider lending some of those much-needed funds or before becoming a silent equity business partner entitled to some share of profits should the business meet expectations.

Try to envision your desired lifestyle for the future. What do you want to spend your time doing? What type of house do you want to live in? It is important to ask yourself these questions. Many of us, as we enjoy one primary source of income from our jobs and occupations become somewhat complacent. It is very rare to find people achieving their financial goals and dreams through their salaries alone; one usually needs alternative sources of income to be able to increase one's wealth in any significant way.

We all have a choice of either spending today or saving up to be able to consume more tomorrow. It will not be easy, and of course, the state of your personal finances, family situation and lifestyle will determine how much you can afford to put away each month. The usual pulls on your income and the temptation to be lured by peer pressure to spend will continue. It is only through discipline and consistency that you can commit to saving something, no matter how small, each month. Through the power of compounding, even small amounts of savings today can grow into significant sums in a few years. Start building passive income today!

P

Philanthropy

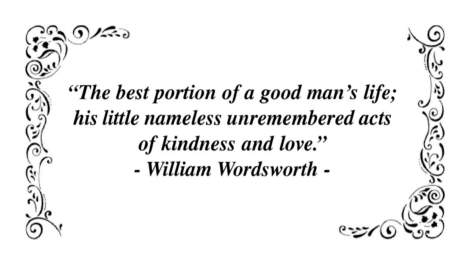

"*The best portion of a good man's life;*
his little nameless unremembered acts
of kindness and love."
- William Wordsworth -

There are certain words that come to mind when you talk about philanthropy; charity, giving, community, doing good and social impact.

The definition of a philanthropist is "someone who donates his or her time, money, and (or) reputation to charitable causes." Charitable giving fulfills a need and usually involves providing food, shelter, clothing, medical care to those in need. Philanthropic giving on the other hand, is more than just a donation and tends to focus on addressing long-term problems; for example, one might invest in the provision of vocational or entrepreneurship training to address a chronic unemployment problem.

Philanthropy affords one the opportunity and privilege of making a positive impact in society. By giving to community, arts, cultural, sports, religious and civic organisations, we can be deliberately involved in causes that we believe in. Foundations are usually established as the vehicle to facilitate philanthropic efforts.

"Impact Investing" a profit-oriented philanthropy, comes with the notion that a positive return on investment can be a powerful tool for social change. Instead of just making money, you are making money and also making an impact at the same time.

Determine what causes you would like to support. What problems, issues, philosophies do you identify with? In the early stages of your philanthropy, you might have a wide array of issues that concern you. Will you support with a one-off donation or commit to give year-on-year? Narrow your choices down to a few initiatives whose ethos and mission are in consonance with your own core values. You are more likely to achieve greater results by being strategic in your giving than if you support too many causes without any real focus.

Before parting with any money, it is important to do some research. One assumes that most charitable groups are credible but there are unscrupulous groups who parade themselves philanthropic organisations. There ought to be some measure of follow up to track results and to see the positive impact of your contribution; this will make it easier for you to continue to give.

Select a few opportunities for your giving and consider partnering with others that are more experienced. As you develop your philanthropic interest, a pilot will afford you with a real learning opportunity to make an impact in areas that you care about; it enables one to think and plan strategically and therefore be more efficient, effective and most importantly, sustainable.

Sometimes one reminisces about how far standards have fallen at ones alma mater or observes with frustration educational institutions badly in need of attention. With an endowed gift, you can provide permanent support for an educational institution. Your contributions will be invested and each year a distribution made to fund the program or area that matches your area of particular interest or focus. You may also decide to, through the title, forever link your name or that of a family member to continued excellence at the college. There are many ways to give. Consider gifts of carefully selected investments in stocks or mutual funds that should continue to give well into the future.

Giving does not mean that you must give only financially; the possibilities of giving of your time, experience, talent and intellect are vast and by sharing your knowledge with others you can add value to your community in many ways.

Having money or means comes with significant responsibility because it makes it possible for you have a positive impact on others. Material possessions will eventually lose their shine, but through philanthropy, one can help others, shape or even save lives. By deciding to make a difference in people's lives, you can bring so much more meaning, value and a lasting form of happiness to your own.

Q

Quick Money

"There is no magic formula for investing. Successful investing requires a well-thought-out-plan, focus, patience, and discipline."
- A-Z Of Personal Finance -

Quick Money

The prospect of accumulating substantial wealth quickly and with minimal effort can be quite appealing. Indeed there are legitimate ways to accumulate substantial amounts of money in a relatively short period of time, but these usually come with substantial risks and lots of luck. Every day there are people who suddenly get rich by winning the lottery, hitting the jackpot on a gambling machine, or betting on a particular stock that skyrocketed. They were lucky.

Greed and Investing

The last global financial crisis brought the issue of greed to the fore. Greed can be defined as "an excessive desire to acquire or possess more," especially more material wealth; greed is about excessive want.

When it comes to investing, far too many people tend to follow the crowd and invest in the latest fad; this can prove to be disastrous, as such investments usually carry an extremely high degree of risk and are unsuitable for most of us. Adverts and rhetoric will show people making huge amounts of money to entice the "greedy" onlooker who then jumps on the band wagon and loses his or her shirt.

The Raging Bull

Greed strikes most investors during a bull market. You feel that you can't bear to ignore the golden opportunity, in case you might miss out. Following the crowd, however, especially if it has already done very well, can have a disastrous effect on your finances. When you are in the middle of an awesome bull run and can literally "feel" the paper profit running through your fingers, it is easy to be overwhelmed by greed. Your most carefully articulated financial plan flies out the window. Many investors are lured into the promise of quick gains and expect to turn hundreds into thousands in just a few months.

Who could have known that stock prices would rise so high and so quickly? Naturally, it would seem ridiculous to get out when you could make so much more money by hanging in there for just a few more weeks. You can almost visualise the new car parked in the garage and your mortgage paid off in one fell swoop! And then suddenly, even quicker than it went up, it comes crashing down. It is amazing how fast "paper profits" can disappear.

Greedy investors tend to be impatient and unrealistic. They throw caution to the wind and "invest" based on vague, subjective information, tips, hype and rumor with the hope of a quick windfall rather than with informed due diligence in pursuing a carefully crafted plan. This usually means the investor often doesn't understand the nature of his or her investments and tends to assume only the best for that investment, often failing to spot any sign of trouble. The investor has usually spent the paper profit before it becomes real.

Seek professional advice, particularly where you don't have the time or expertise to manage your own investments and an appropriate investment plan can be structured for you. If your goals are long-term and you can accommodate a degree of risk in your investing, the stock market would be an appropriate option. However, if you need your money fairly soon, you should limit the risk you take and increase your exposure to cash and other fixed income securities.

Avoid Get-Rich-Quick Schemes

Many anxious investors seek opportunities to recover quickly from the catastrophic losses in their portfolios. This makes them particularly vulnerable to get-rich-quick schemes. In many of these schemes, only a few people make money, and everyone else loses their entire investment. Sadly those who fall for scams such as pyramid and other such schemes can hardly afford to. In most cases it is greed that is taken advantage of and this rarely brings long-term success.

Be careful. There is no magic formula for investing. Successful investing requires a well-thought-out-plan, focus, patience and discipline. Successful investors aren't looking for a miracle; they are more realistic and seek steady ways to improve their performance over time in a rational manner rather than latching onto a get-rich-quick opportunity.

It is tempting to try to get rich quickly, but the process of getting rich slowly and steadily via saving and long-term investing is tested and reliable. Don't let wishful thinking cloud your better judgement; if something sounds too good to be true, it probably is too good to be true.

R

Retirement

"After several years of hard work, your retirement years should be one of your most rewarding life stages and an opportunity to fulfil the dreams that you finally have the time to pursue, free from routine constraints."
- A-Z Of Personal Finance -

R

Retirement

Are You Prepared for Retirement?

How would you like to spend your retirement years? Will your nest egg be able to provide the kind of lifestyle that you have become accustomed to, and how much will it cost you?

Sadly, many people end up impoverished in their later years or are totally dependent on their children or other family members. Other retirees, however, are redefining retirement as an exciting time to explore new interests. No longer the end of the work life, retirement has become a new beginning, often the start of a new career, world travel, going back to school, starting a new business venture, spending more time with family, or engaging in high-impact philanthropic endeavours that can change lives.

Here are some scenarios to consider as you plan for your retirement:

- Playing several rounds of daily golf may be one of your goals; or it could be travelling, spending more time with your children and grandchildren, or pottering around the garden. At last you can take your passion or hobby to a new level and maybe even build a business out of it. If you have never had time for a hobby or a new vocation, retirement may offer you a chance to take one up.

- You might want to "give back" to your community by volunteering at your church or at a non-profit organisation. Philanthropy may open a new world to you. You might want to go back to school just to learn about a subject you've always been interested in. Or do you want to share the immense knowledge and experience that you have garnered over so many years by teaching?

The possibilities are endless; ideally this should be the time of your life where you can open yourself up to new and exciting opportunities to keep you productive, mentally stimulated and fulfilled. Yet, for many people, an uncertain future clouds these rosy pictures and they may never become a reality without adequate preparation.

How Much Money Will You Need?

Most people are aware of the importance of pensions and retirement planning. Pensions, whilst they are an important part of retirement income, will very rarely cover all your financial needs if you wish to maintain a certain standard of living during your retirement years. Your retirement income should be supplemented with income from other personal savings and investments.

Everyone's retirement goals are unique and a function of their own age, stage and financial situation. As life spans grow longer worldwide, it is not unusual nowadays to spend over 20 years in retirement, you need to be sure that your financial resources can last as long as you do. If you were to retire at 60 and then lived for at least another 20 years, how much income would you need for each year of your retirement, and how much do you have to save now to generate that kind of income to afford the lifestyle you desire?

How Much Risk Can You Afford to Take?

Your investment portfolio should be tailored to reflect your age, the amount of money you have and will need. Inflation and market volatility have forced investors to face the reality of their financial position. With the specter of inflation always lurking, and the possibility of spending more than two decades in retirement, your investment earnings will need to keep pace in order for you to have any chance of maintaining your current standard of living.

The type of investments you make play an important role in how much you would have saved at retirement. A diversified portfolio of cash, bonds, stocks and real estate will help to protect you from investment risk. You don't want all your retirement funds invested in high-risk investments, for in spite of the higher yields this might generate, you need to balance risk and return in order to achieve your goals. The asset allocation will largely depend on your risk tolerance and how long you have until your retirement. As you move closer to retirement your investments choices tend to become more conservative and geared more towards income generating options.

Health is Wealth

Whilst we all pray that we will enjoy good health in our later years, the reality of declining health as we age should be addressed seriously in retirement planning. Even the most elaborate retirement savings and investment plans can be decimated if you find yourself with health challenges and without adequate health insurance in place. It takes just one major illness to wipe out several years of saving and investing. No matter how healthy you are currently, build a financial cushion that allows for unexpected expenses and do not ignore obtaining health insurance. The endless opportunities in retirement can only be attained if you have saved and invested wisely and have remained fairly healthy.

Your current income is a good starting point for calculating your retirement savings needs. Experts estimate that most people will need between 65 and 80 percent of current income to maintain their current lifestyle when they retire. Online retirement calculators are available; these are useful tools to help you estimate how much you will need in retirement.

Start Early

In your 20s and 30s, retirement seems a lifetime away; but it's never too early to start planning for it right from the start – with your first job. Those who start saving for retirement in their 20s have a better chance of building a large nest egg and achieving sustained financial success. Saving even a small amount on a regular basis can add up to a tidy sum over a long period of time. If you are young with retirement still decades away, and with fewer responsibilities, you can afford to assume more risk and can ride out the inevitable market volatility of the stock market to achieve higher returns over the long-term.

Educate Yourself

Financial security and knowledge are closely linked. It is important to have a broad understanding of basic investment principles, how you save is just as important as how much you save. Educate yourself on the different savings options available and what might work for you and seek professional advice to guide you. Monitor and review your savings and investments over time to ensure that they are still appropriate for you.

Enjoy Your Retirement

After several years of hard work, your retirement years should be one of your most rewarding life stages and an opportunity to fulfil the dreams that you finally have the time to pursue, free from routine constraints. Today, the responsibility for building your nest egg and ensuring that it supports you for the rest of your life rests squarely on your shoulders. Make saving for retirement a priority and start now.

R

Risk

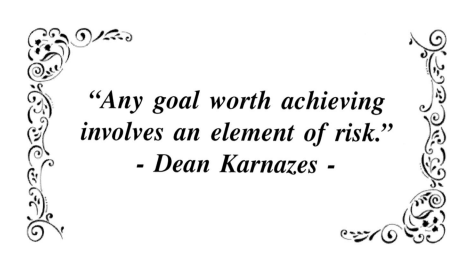

"Any goal worth achieving
involves an element of risk."
- Dean Karnazes -

Risk

W hat is your attitude to risk? What would you do in these situations?

You have a long overdue vacation planned. Two weeks before your departure, you lose your job. Would you?

a. Cancel your vacation?
b. Make plans for a shorter, cheaper vacation instead?
c. Go on holiday as planned, you'd better just enjoy yourself now and think about job hunting later.
d. Go on an extended vacation. This might be your last opportunity for a long time!

A stock you bought just six months ago has suddenly increased in value by over 40%. What would you do?

a. It was always a long-term investment so you will continue to just hold

b. You are certain it will keep going up so you borrow money and buy more of the stock

c. Sell part of it now and move your profit to a low risk investment

Risk is a fundamental part of investing. It is the possibility that an investment will lose value. Is inflation eating away at your life savings in a bank account, because you are too scared of the stock market? Do you hear of the greatest opportunity of a lifetime and stake everything for it? Or, do you just sit back and do nothing?

The concept of risk tolerance, assumes that your ability to endure risk is a reflection of your personality and feelings about taking chances. Your investment style to a large extent depends on your age, your life stage, your personality, your time horizon and your financial position; it determines the types of investments that may be suited to you. If you can't sleep at night because you are worrying about your investments, you have probably assumed too much risk.

Are you a conservative or risk-averse investor? Are you a moderate investor, who wants to protect your principle while achieving modest growth? Or are you an aggressive investor who will confront risk head-on with the expectation of greater returns?

Risk and Reward

Understanding the relationship between risk and reward is an important part of investing. Generally, the higher the risk, the higher the potential return. If you are unwilling to take at least some investment risk, then be prepared to accept low returns. Your goal should be to maximise returns without taking on more risk than you can bear.

Over the course of the past few years we have had some hard lessons in risk. Sometimes investment success looks so certain that the thought of limiting any rewards with a strategy seems ridiculous, but jumping into markets fully exposed can leave you badly burnt. Here are some classic strategies that will help you to manage risk.

"Don't Put all Your Eggs in one Basket"

Without being pessimistic, it is important to be conscious of the fact that unexpected and unfortunate events do happen. You could find yourself suddenly out of a job, or you or a member of your family could suddenly face an unplanned expense such as a large medical bill. If an emergency occurs and you don't have enough money to cover immediate expenses, you will probably have to dip into your savings and investments for cash. If your car loan is due you could lose your vehicle or be forced to borrow more money.

An emergency fund is provides a safety net against unexpected expenses and makes it less likely for you to have sell investments prematurely or having to borrow at expensive rates to meet an urgent need.

Diversification spreads your risk across various investments. If you put all your money in one investment, your return will depend solely on the performance of that investment. The more diversified your portfolio is, however, the lower the impact of a decline in one investment will be. Mutual funds provide the benefit of instant diversification.

What is the Appropriate Asset Mix for You?

An asset allocation strategy is based on the premise that the various asset classes, such as stocks, money market accounts and cash perform differently. It looks at your particular goals, your age and circumstances and helps to determine an appropriate asset mix for you.

Stocks, for instance, offer the highest returns across these three classes over the long term, but carry the most risk. If you invest funds that you need for next terms school fees in the stock market, you may be forced to sell the investment to raise cash at a time when the investment is at a loss. Bonds may not be as lucrative, but offer more stability than stocks. Money market returns whilst they may be low, provide fixed income and offer the relative safety of your initial investment.

There is a natural tendency to buy stocks when prices are rising and stop buying when there is a downturn. Cost averaging encourages you to buy more stock when prices are low and fewer when prices are high. It is a particularly useful tool in a volatile market as you can reduce the average cost of your shares.

The fear of losing money is one of the greatest psychological obstacles to building wealth. All investments carry a certain amount of risk so the question isn't whether or not to take risks; it is about how much risk you are comfortable with, given your own particular circumstance. Remember, to earn the highest return, you must assume some degree of risk. So choose wisely and don't ignore your gut instinct.

S

Savings

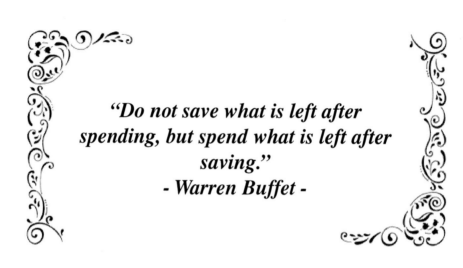

"Do not save what is left after spending, but spend what is left after saving."
- Warren Buffet -

Savings

Life is full of uncertainties, so it is important to set aside some savings, a cushion, to alleviate the shock of a completely unexpected event that can lead to unplanned expenses.

A n American research report found that 47 percent of workers surveyed were living paycheck to paycheck and 25 percent of those surveyed had no savings at all. It appears that too many people are choosing to live for today rather than save for an unpredictable and unknown tomorrow. Even highly-paid executives have no savings or investments whatsoever and live in a state of oblivion to the reality of what happens when they are no longer in their company's employ.

Godfrey is 52 years old and is an executive in a telecom company. He lives in company accommodation with his family. Their four-bedroom well-appointed apartment comes with a swimming pool, a children's play area, a gym, tennis and squash courts, a water-treatment plant and a generator. Godfrey is entitled to two company cars, both with drivers. His "perks" also include three business-class tickets a year to Europe, company medical insurance for him and his family, and he employs a cook, a steward, a laundry man and a nanny. The couple have three children; Betty is enrolled at an international school and Bessie and Dennis are at a boarding school in England. Godfrey prefers that his wife not work so that she has time with the children and can travel frequently for school events and mid-term breaks.

Godfrey has eight years to retirement. He has not been very disciplined about saving and investing and since the company takes care of everything, this hasn't really been a problem. He plans to acquire a plot of land in due course and hopes to build on it so that his family can move into their own home before he retires at age 60. A global economic crisis has affected the fortunes of the company and it must downsize; Godfrey is on the list of those to be laid off.

Nowadays the news is full of stories of doom and gloom; from floods following severe storms, job loss, a health event, a fire and so on. While no one really has control over the future, you can make an effort to prepare for the aftermath by having access to some savings to protect you and your family. Far too many people have not planned ahead for the events that happen in our lives and are completely unprepared for a financial crisis. They have no savings at all, they don't have any insurance and go through life just hoping or assuming that someone else will cover the bills for them. Whilst you may be lucky to have access to such funds, most people will find that there isn't anyone out there that they can completely rely upon. No matter how meticulous or organised you are about your personal finances, emergencies do occur when you least expect them and can disrupt your budget so severely that it can take you several months or even years to recover.

The Need for an Emergency Fund

Do you have any money set aside for a "rainy day?" How much are you saving? Remember that life is full of uncertainties, so it is important to set aside a sum of money, a cushion, to alleviate the shock of a completely unexpected event that leads to unplanned expenses. Major car or home repairs, a faulty generator or the more serious events such as a sudden job loss, a medical emergency, or a death in the family feel even worse when there isn't enough cash in place to take care of them. An emergency fund will help you deal with such situations if and when they arise.

Where Should You Keep the Money?

It is important that the emergency fund is placed in an account that you can easily draw from without restrictions or penalties. Keeping money in an easy-access account takes discipline, so avoid using a current account to build your savings, as you will be tempted to dip into it to settle your day-to-day bills and expenses. The most common places to park emergency funds are savings accounts and money market deposits. Consider setting up a savings account at your bank and having the money automatically transferred into your savings account on a regular basis. Such automated savings are not only convenient, but they can grow significantly over time.

As far as possible, your emergency savings vehicle should be risk free. Whilst it is important to shop around for competitive interest rates on your deposit, always remember that the primary consideration should be the safety of your funds and not the highest rate of return. Such funds should not be invested in the stock market because there will be the inevitable short-term market volatility; if you have a sudden need for cash you don't want to be forced to sell shares at a loss.

How Much Should You Save?

If you don't have any savings at all, the key is to start with a small amount. This will take some time to grow but will encourage you to develop a savings habit; over time you can slowly start to increase your contribution to your fund. A generally accepted rule of thumb is that an emergency fund should be able to cover three to six months of living expenses.

Naturally, the appropriate amount that one should hold will vary from person to person. Depending on your particular circumstance, your family situation, your debt profile and the type of insurance cover you maintain will determine what amount makes sense for you. Some people will feel more secure with more money set aside than others. More serious life-threatening emergencies should have been addressed by having the appropriate insurance policies in place.

If you are seriously in debt, it doesn't make sense to keep a large amount of savings where the interest on your debt is higher than what you are receiving on your deposit. Whether you are in debt or not, however, you do need some savings you can rely on rather than having to resort to even more borrowing. Besides, it is far easier to simply withdraw from your deposit account than to have to arrange credit at short notice and significant cost.

Guard your emergency fund carefully. You should not be dipping into it for incidental expenses; use it only in the event of a completely unexpected crisis or an emergency. If and when you are forced to dip into it, make every effort to replenish it quickly so that it is always available when you need it. Just knowing you have that reserve fund to help you cope during these challenging times will give you some peace of mind. With emergency savings and insurance you won't be as anxious should something go wrong.

Whilst is important to have some savings, by far the most important consideration is your overall financial flexibility, what resources you can muster to help you withstand a crisis, even where it is unexpectedly severe or long-lasting.

S

Speculation

"A prediction about the direction of the stock market tells you nothing about where stocks are headed, but a whole lot about the person making the prediction."
- Warren Buffet -

S

Speculation

Investing Versus Speculating

When you buy stock, are you buying as a speculator, a long-term investor or as a long-term investor who can't resist the temptation to speculate just once in a while? Most people think that at the moment they are buying stock they are investors; but how many are really investors and not speculators. In hindsight, it is clear that in the midst of the last bull market many of us thought we were investors; having seen our "paper profits" evaporate, we are now coming to terms with the fact that much of the time there was some speculation in our decision making.

Far too many of us are really habitual gamblers who dive into markets and bet on stock based on the slightest rumour, gossip and hype, hoping to get rich with a stroke of luck. If you plan to gamble, it makes better sense to go to a casino or to buy a lottery ticket and take your chances; you might just get lucky; these pastimes as were specifically created for this purpose.

It is important to know who you are and how you intend to participate in the stock market if you are going to make any real success of it. Knowing if you are an investor or a speculator is essential for developing an appropriate investment strategy for yourself. The mindset, attitude and behaviour of an investor, speculator, or the gambler, are vastly different.

The Investor

An investor, through careful analysis of a company, determines what it is worth and seeks to buy stock that is trading at a discount to its intrinsic or true value. The investor looks at the value that may accrue over time, as the particular stock price is affected by the ongoing business, the sector, the economy and of course market perception. Investment decisions are thus based largely on factual information, detailed research and little emotion.

Through the purchase of stocks, real estate, currency, commodities and other assets the investor is willing to take on a moderate degree of risk in the hope of achieving long-term capital gain. Investors often have a fundamental "buy and hold" approach and are interested in long-term investments that provide a steady source of passive income. Typically, an investor is less concerned about the daily market fluctuation.

Investing in its truest sense is putting money into something and leaving it there for the long-term. By using this technique with stocks, investors can collect dividends that provide consistent income over time. Over several years, an investor that sticks with the stock of a company that routinely pays a dividend will usually come out ahead. Similarly, purchasing property in an attractive location that has enjoyed consistent capital appreciation is also a good investment.

The Speculator

Benjamin Graham, a British-born American economist and professional investor, once described speculation as "a rat race of trying to get the highest possible return in the shortest period of time". Speculators are willing to take large, but calculated risks in search of large rewards over a short time period. Speculators buy, hold and sell stock, commodities, futures, currencies, real estate, or any valuable financial instrument, not on the basis of careful analysis or for income through interest, rent, or dividends, but rather in anticipation of profiting from market fluctuations. Speculators are prepared to accept calculated risk in the hope of making attractive potential returns quickly.

Whilst investors use diversification as part of a strategy to spread their risk, speculators often invest heavily in one market sector, one that is showing an upward trend. This means that as a speculator you would sell at just the right time to make a profit. It is not easy to predict when the market in question will peak. A speculator may wait too long, and the market may crash before he or she can get out. This obviously results in substantial losses.

Some people view speculation as gambling. Professional speculators are rather like professional gamblers. Some people gamble for a living, taking calculated risks with large sums, seeking to maximise their edge with sophisticated techniques and skill. They are usually fully aware of the risk involved and are schooled in managing such risk in the most efficient manner possible.

Is it wrong to speculate? There is nothing wrong with speculating; indeed many people speculate in one part of their portfolio and invest in another. The problem arises when speculating becomes foolhardy, that is, when the "lay investors" confuse investing with speculating, unaware of the real risks, or perhaps ignoring them altogether. They buy stock based on hot tips and rumor and lacking proper knowledge and skill, risk more money than they can afford to lose. A few make fortunes but the inept ones, sadly the majority, lose heavily. It can be perilous to venture into the financial markets blindly.

When speculating becomes rampant, it creates a situation that cannot be sustained. Whilst speculators buy securities based sometimes on little more than whims, they also dump stocks with abandon. As a result, stocks may become significantly overvalued when everyone is excited and involved, and grossly undervalued when the bear-run takes over.

The bright side for those who have not totally given up on the stock market is that the very speculative behaviour that helped create the "bubble" creates an opportunity for investors to pick up companies that are undervalued. Inevitably, the market will continue to be volatile and could even go down further in the short-term.

Both investing and speculating do work. The key is to know which game you are playing and not to let emotion cloud your judgement. Do note however that while it can be profitable in the short-term, particularly during bull markets, speculating seldom provides a lifetime of steady income or returns. It should thus be left only to those who truly understand what they are doing and have weighed and are comfortable with the significant risk involved.

T

Talent

"You can only become truly accomplished at something you love. Don't make money your goal. Instead, pursue the things you love doing, and then do them so well that people can't take their eyes off you."
- Maya Angelou -

T

Talent

Don't rest on your laurels; be creative – think outside the box. Identify your strengths, skills, and talents and do something with them.

Are you struggling to make ends meet? If so, you are not alone. The high cost of living has prompted many people to seek for other ways to earn extra income and still hold on to a full-time job. For all of us, a diversification of earnings is advisable. Not only does it boost your earnings, but it also provides a safety net should you experience salary delays, a salary reduction, unexpected job loss, or some other financial setback such as major unplanned expenses or significant losses in investments.

Have You Identified Your Talents?

Research shows that most successful people earn multiple streams of revenue primarily from rental income from real estate investments, interest and dividend income from investments in the financial markets and businesses. Even if you do not have the money to invest in the financial markets, real estate, or business, other avenues exist to supplement your income.

There are different types of people; there are those capable people who are prepared to face the indignities and the consequences of earning a low income or no income at all, whereas there are others who are determined and proactive about making efforts to improve their lot and lead a better life by thinking outside the box and seeking extra income by utilising their talents and skills.

Most people have some inherent talent or skill that if properly nurtured, can create a huge window of opportunity that will not only help them earn but will also give them a sense of fulfillment and happiness. Don't just rest on your laurels; be creative – think outside the box. Identify your strengths, talents and skills and do something with them. Which one of them can you take immediate action on?

A potential freelance job or business should incorporate the skills and talents you already possess. Ideally it should require a relatively small amount of your time and require low oversight, be fairly low risk and not require a huge capital outlay. Above all it must be customer-centric and deliver a high level of service and it must be unique.

So, What Can You do?

Are you a communicator? Are you an organiser? Are you a budding entrepreneur? Here are just a few self-help examples of what some enterprising people have embarked upon as they faced the predicament of unemployment or low income. They have effectively utilised their hobbies and talents, often resulting in the establishing of viable businesses that subsequently became their primary source of income.

Private Tutoring

Several schools have proved inadequate in equipping children for significant examinations without additional support from private tutors. Further, parents often do not have the time or inclination to tutor their children, particularly during the long holidays, which creates huge demand for such services to keep children academically engaged.

Can you teach someone to speak properly? Do you have an exceptional skill in a particular academic subject or language? Are you a gifted musician or do you have an exceptional skill in a particular sport? If you possess the deep knowledge and skills and the ability to start a tutoring service in a particular subject, or skill, there may be an opportunity to supplement your income.

Computer Skills

Computers and the internet have become an integral part of our lives. Clearly, those with strong computer skills can seek to offer services in web designing, programming and trouble-shooting. Individuals and businesses are often in need of high-quality presentations for marketing purposes, and skills in the design of power point presentations are highly sought after.

Cooking and Baking

Do family and friends often compliment you on your outstanding culinary skills? If you are a good cook and enjoy cooking, you can consider giving cookery classes or offering catering services at small events and parties. If you are good at baking, you can start by taking orders for birthday cakes and other special occasions. There is some demand for cakes and bakes or freshly made sandwiches delivered to local businesses during the lunch hour.

Arts and Crafts

If you have creative talents, ideas and the ability to work with your hands and are passionate about what you do, you can turn your passion into a profitable, part-time, income earning opportunity. Sewing, jewelry making, artwork, novel crafts such as candle or soap making are much sought after particularly during the holiday season when people are looking for gifts.

Home Repair Services

Every homeowner needs the help of someone to do repairs as and when they occur. Some people are very good at do-it-yourself solutions but unfortunately most do not have the confidence, the tools, or the time to do it successfully. As we are all too aware, it is increasingly difficult to find reliable and efficient workers, and technicians to do the most basic repairs. If you have such skills and are service oriented and have credible referees, you can offer your services to households in a niche area.

Don't Jeopardise Your Day Job

Be careful not to jeopardise your current employment income by being distracted and losing focus. You owe your employer your full attention so don't let any other interests eat into your work time. The key is to keep them separate yet be well organised so that your side job doesn't interfere with your regular role and vice versa. It is important to ensure that there is no conflict of interest. It often helps if you are in partnership so that you and your partner(s) can cover for each other as your business evolves.

Whilst these efforts on a small scale will not make you rich overnight, you can certainly create some useful extra income this way. Even in difficult times you can acquire certain skills or build on your existing skills. The independence and confidence that you derive from less dependency on an employer opens up a wide vista of options, enabling you to experiment with new opportunities and have a better chance at long-term financial stability and success.

T

Trusts

"Trusts are a valuable tool, but they may not be for everyone. It pays to know the ins and outs before you put your trust in a trust."
- Ted Miller -

Trusts

A will or a trust? Which one is for you? You have worked hard for your money and it is hoped, you have made every attempt to save and invest conscientiously. Naturally you want some control over what happens to your assets after you pass on. Whether you are a person of modest means or otherwise, if you have an estate, and if you are financially prepared, you will be making life easier for those you leave behind.

A living trust is a popular alternative to the traditional last will and testament, which is the most basic document in any estate plan; but it is important to understand their differences, as well as the pros and cons of each to determine which will best suit your particular circumstances. Consider some of these issues as you decide on what to adopt as part of your estate plan.

Holding and Managing Assets

Phillip Babson owns an investment portfolio consisting of stocks and mutual funds worth about $200,000, a family home and other commercial property, and two cars. He created a living trust and transferred all his assets into it, naming his wife Isabella and their 12-year-old twins, Gaby and Andrew, as beneficiaries. When he passed away, the trust property automatically passed to Isabella and the children. As the children were minors the trust deed stipulated that the trustee was responsible for providing Isabella with an annual income and would also pay for the children's education up to the masters degree level. In addition the trust would manage the twins' assets until they were 30 years old, after which trust assets would be equally distributed to the three beneficiaries.

A will comes into play only after your demise, whilst a living trust takes effect during your lifetime. A trust thus puts in place a mechanism to hold and manage your property both before and after your death and stipulates how those assets, as well as any trust income, are distributed thereafter. Whilst a will alone cannot hold assets, it can make the provision that any property in your estate at the time of your death automatically becomes a part of the trust. This is particularly useful where there is a need to hold and manage assets for young beneficiaries or to protect beneficiaries with special needs. Assets that have not already been transferred to the trust at the time of death will be subject to probate unless a supplementary will has been made at the time that the trust was established. Probate is the legal process in which ownership of property is transferred from the deceased estate to his or her heirs.

Guardianship

A will lays down all your wishes as to who should look after your minor children in the event of your death. The guardian's legal responsibility is to provide for their welfare. Unlike a will, a living trust cannot designate a legal guardian for minor children; you would be required to add a "pour-over will" as a supplement to the trust where such a provision can be made.

Costs

Setting up a will is much simpler and much cheaper than setting up a trust, but the probate process can become expensive, depending on the size of the estate. Every day families pay out huge parts of their inheritance due to probate costs and estate taxes. You have an obligation to protect and preserve what you have spent years accumulating and a properly drafted trust can help to minimise taxes.

The set-up cost for a living trust and the annual management fees can make it an expensive estate- planning vehicle; indeed a trust really only makes sense where there are significant assets involved and the added cost and complexity of the arrangements make it worthwhile.

The Probate Process

Probate is unavoidable with a will and can take several months and, in some instances, even years to administer. Keeping assets out of probate could save your heirs much time and money. Since a living trust comes into effect as soon as it is funded, assets cannot be frozen, which means that your family has immediate access to funds as needed and can avoid some of the challenges associated with probate. This applies to assets that are transferred to the trust during your lifetime.

Privacy

When a will goes through probate it becomes a public document, and anyone can gain access to it and read it. A trust protects your privacy, as it is not subject to probate and thus does not become a matter of public record. This can make it more difficult for disgruntled heirs or relations or other beneficiaries from challenging the distribution of your assets and can minimise the likelihood of litigation. This can be particularly important for very large estates with complicated family arrangements.

A trust tends to be better equipped to deal with creditors and long-lost relatives who show up to stake a claim to the assets.

Seek Professional Advice

A will and a living trust can work in tandem to create a seamless estate plan. It is important to seek professional advice to determine which is the most appropriate for you. Trusts are more complex and require much greater detail to ensure that you are as precise as possible and leave no room for misinterpretation.

For some, a living trust is a very practical tool and is ideal; yet for others, it may be a waste of time and money. Whether or not one or the other is for you, will largely be determined by your personal circumstances, the type of assets you own and the size of your estate. Whichever you choose, you will have peace of mind in knowing that all you have worked for will go to the people or the causes most dear to your heart.

U

Unemployment

"I do not believe we can repair the basic fabric of society until people who are willing to work have work. Work organizes life. It gives structure and discipline to life."
- Bill Clinton -

Unemployment

Job loss ranks as one of life's most challenging events. Some of the issues involved include adjusting your finances, looking for a new job and coping with the emotional and social impact of your situation. It would be much easier to deal with it financially and emotionally if you've prepared for the worst by planning ahead but even if you failed to anticipate this sudden change in your circumstances, here are some practical steps to take if you find yourself unemployed:

Don't Panic

When you think about all the bills and monthly expenses you have to face without a steady income, it is easy to despair. Try to remain calm and do not rush into any major financial decisions whilst you assess your situation; you need a clear, positive outlook. Even if you are eligible, be cautious about dipping into your retirement savings account.

Do you have any savings? How much money have you saved? How long will it last based on your monthly bills? The importance of an emergency fund becomes glaring in situations like this. If you have been able to set aside, say, six months of income in a high-yield money market account, you will be able to pay some of your bills and relieve some of the financial stress while you look for a new job. But if you have always lived from month to month, this may not be an option.

What are Your Entitlements?

What do your full entitlements amount to? If you have no savings at all and you are fortunate enough to receive severance pay or other benefits, use this as a bridge to tide you over the difficult period. Spend carefully, and do not use all of your entitlements to make large payments, such as to pay your mortgage, as you might have to live off that money for what could be an extended period of time. Don't let such funds lull you into complacency; you need to actively seek a new job or other income-generating opportunities.

Revise Your Budget

How best can you adjust your budget to suit your new circumstances? Develop a new written budget that will cover several months of unemployment based on what you have saved and any expected income. How much will it cost to maintain your family, your home and your lifestyle? Keep your family members fully in the picture so that they too can adjust their expectations about what you can afford. You will have to control your spending by cutting back on non-essential expenses. Naturally your priority will be for housing, food and utility bills. Of major concern would be the lack of access to affordable insurance and appropriate healthcare. These must also be planned for.

Be Cautious About Borrowing

It is tempting for credit card holders to start to load day-to-day expenses on their cards. Try to avoid doing this except when absolutely necessary and only for critically important expenses that cannot be delayed.

Making on additional debt can keep you in denial about your true financial situation and make things worse.

If you are unable to fulfill your financial obligations, such as paying your mortgage or repaying a car loan, contact your lenders immediately, and inform them that you have lost your job and are actively seeking new employment. It may be possible to negotiate new terms and come to an arrangement to adjust your payments for a limited period of time. It is better to approach them upfront rather than fall behind with your payments. If you default on your home or vehicle loan, your bank will take steps to repossess your property.

Stay Socially Connected

Some people feel embarrassed or inadequate after losing a job. Don't withdraw and let negative feelings stop you from taking important steps; you need your network composed of professionals and non-professionals now more than ever before. Reach out to family, friends, ex-colleagues, people within your network, and spread the word that you are in the job market. By seeking support you may find they are aware of new opportunities for you. Your CV should be regularly updated and circulated.

Seek Alternative Sources of Income

With the sheer number of people currently searching for work, you need to cast your net wide, and not just for the same type of job. Don't pigeonhole yourself into a specific role or job. Be practical and flexible so you can increase your chances of finding work. Consider temporary or part-time work that will generate income and give you the time and flexibility to attend job interviews and actively pursue a more permanent position. This might be a time to upgrade your skills or to go back to school, which would help to create an impressive resume.

If you have alternate sources of income, you will be in a much more comfortable position should you lose your job. Your hobbies, talents and skills, and other interests may be converted to a business and offer serious possibilities for income.

Be Positive

Apart from the financial issues associated with job loss, there are usually emotional and personal aspects that are too often ignored. Whether yours was the only position that was cut, or an entire unit or department, the feelings caused by being laid off are largely the same regardless of the circumstances. Many people experience a loss of self-esteem, a sense of failure and even depression after retrenchment. But it's important to take your next steps based on clear rational thought, devoid of emotion.

As difficult as this may sound, one should try to view this period of unemployment as a positive event, an opportunity to re-evaluate your future and, potentially, change your career or start a new business. Losing your employment may well be the impetus you need to take a fresh look at your life and to redefine your goals. Often, it is times like this that propel people to greater heights.

V

Volatility

"A stock market decline is as routine as a January blizzard in Colorado. If you're prepared, it can't hurt you. A decline is a great opportunity to pick up the bargains left behind by investors who are fleeing the storm in panic."
- Peter Lynch -

V

Volatility

Managing Your Money in Turbulent Times

As you listen to the financial news each day on the radio and television, your survival instincts are probably urging you to get out of the market now before things get even worse. This reaction is not totally unfounded, as for several months there might be nothing but doom and gloom, and no financial expert is willing or able to tell you convincingly exactly when things will really start to turn around convincingly.

What was the reason why you were investing in the first place, assuming you didn't just dive in and jump on the wagon without any real financial plan or goal in mind? You are probably thinking that the market fell just when you were smiling at your paper profits; you thought it would still soar or at least stay stable.

A well-thought-out investment plan that takes into account your risk tolerance, your age and stage in life, and your family considerations will hold you in good stead through market volatility. If you are a long-term investor and your plan reflects this, don't be swayed by short-term market sentiment and derail your plan. It is unwise to get out now. Stick with your plan.

Here a few tips to help you to stay calm in these uncertain times:

Stay Calm

The very worst thing an investor can do is to panic and sell shares at a loss. Volatility is a natural part of the investing cycle, so try to stay calm as markets usually do recover. Stay focused on your long-term goals; if you did have an original plan, it would have taken market volatility into account.

If you were investing for retirement and that is still five to ten years away, then you have lots of time for the markets to recover. Even if you are already in retirement, it is unlikely that you will need all your money within the next few years, so as long as you have enough in pension savings, some cash or other money market deposits to cover your more immediate needs, resist the temptation to sell your stocks or mutual funds at what would be a loss if you were to cash out now.

Try to be patient and take time to make well-considered informed decisions. It is impossible to accurately predict how long a bear market will last, but patient investors are often rewarded as they wait for the market to start to recover. Remember, markets go up and down and when they begin to recover they often do so quite quickly. Some investors panic and sell off their investments during a downturn only to see the market recover soon afterwards. Missing out on this crucial time can have a huge impact on long-term performance.

Watching Day-to-Day Market Movements

It is tempting to constantly watch the market. Unless it is a part of your job or your hobby, staying fixated daily on a turbulent market is not only bad for your financial health if it causes you to panic, but it can also take its toll on your physical health as worry and anxiety set in. Watching the market rise and fall daily can be a form of self-torture. You must know your investment personality and how much risk you can afford to take for your age or disposition. If you can't cope with what the stock pages tell each day and can afford to wait the long haul, stay away.

Diversify

In laymen's terms, diversification means "don't put all your eggs in one basket"; it is an investment technique that builds different types of investments into a single portfolio. The idea is to spread your risk so wide that no one problem will do too much damage. Having a more varied portfolio will help you to better cope with volatility caused by interest rates, inflation, foreign exchange, or political risk. To be diversified across asset classes, sectors, stocks and countries helps to minimise the impact of a downturn.

Cost Averaging

Don't be put off saving because of the lull in the market. Be disciplined and consistent with your saving and investing. By saving regularly and earning interest on your savings, even the smallest amounts can grow substantially. By investing the same amount of money regularly, say every month, regardless of whether the market is up or down, you are saved from investing all your money when the market is at its peak; when prices are low, your money buys more shares or units. Whilst cost averaging does not protect you from losses or assure you profits, it does help you to reduce risk and reduce the average cost of your purchases.

Review Your Portfolio

Even if you are a long-term investor, do not assume that you should just leave your portfolio as it is. It is important to review your portfolio objectives from time to time and certainly when there has been significant change in your life; revisit your financial plan and your portfolio and do a thorough assessment of your financial situation at least once a year. You may need to update or adjust it as appropriate. This will help to keep your asset allocation in line with the amount of risk you are willing and able to take. Furthermore, it ensures that you are still working towards your short- and long-term goals.

Unless your long-term planning was completely inappropriate or you have a cash emergency, you should stay with your overall plan and not be too hasty in changing your asset allocation.

Seek Advice

Even if you're an astute investor, you can still benefit from professional advice. Investment professionals can help you understand how the changing market conditions affect your portfolio and can make recommendations based on a deep knowledge of markets and their vagaries. When it comes down to picking individual investments, an advisor who knows your personal situation can help you articulate your financial goals and pick the investment most appropriate for you at a particular time.

Cash is King

In turbulent times, cash is king. The value of an emergency fund becomes much more apparent, and it is wise to have a cushion to cover 3 – 6 months worth of expenses in a money market account so that if you need money in a hurry, you aren't forced to sell assets at a loss. Manage your cash wisely and do a detailed budget of all your income and expenses. Be prepared to cut back if necessary.

Look at the market decline as a buying opportunity; some stocks may be undervalued and selling at a discount. If you are planning to enter the market now to take advantage of some of the low prices, you must be willing to wait for the long haul; plan to pay less now for significant long-term investments.

Whilst these are trying times for many investors, they provide an opportunity for us all to learn from the times and understand some important lessons about investing. By developing your knowledge and understanding of market risks, you can position yourself for long-term investing success and avoid making costly mistakes in the future. Risk is a very real part of investing, and market movements certainly do take their toll on your nerves; but with the right strategies in place, you can ride the storm with some peace of mind.

W

Weddings

"After the excitement of the wedding ceremonies and all the festivities, be well-prepared to face a financial future together."
- A-Z Of Personal Finance -

Weddings

The announcement of your child or grandchild's engagement and prospective wedding is every parent's dream. You certainly want your loved one to have a dream wedding and support him or her in every way. But planning the wedding can be exciting yet stressful, for as we all know nuptials can be expensive. Whether you are the bride, the groom, the in-laws, the parents, or grandparents, here are a few tips that should help you get through the big day:

Prepare a Budget

It is important to keep the wedding costs under control. A good first step, as you plan for the upcoming wedding, is to determine how much it will all cost. Make a list of everything you can think of that you will need for the engagement ceremony and for the wedding day and an estimate of what each will cost. As you get price quotes, refine your budget and prioritise carefully.

Some of the typical high-cost items that you need to consider include: attire, flowers, hiring the venue, catering at the various events, the décor, the actual ceremonies, the photographer and videographer, the choir and organists as well as other musicians or a DJ, rentals, stationery, gifts, party favors, hotel bookings, the honeymoon and more.

Who Pays for What?

In some cultures, for the traditional and white wedding, protocol is not financially kind to the bride's family, as they are expected to pay for the majority of the wedding costs which is often a huge strain for the father of the bride. Fortunately, times have changed, and it is common practice these days for both sets of parents to contribute. Circumstances, not tradition, now dictate who will pay what for a wedding and it is more about who can afford to foot what can be exorbitant costs. If one family is far better off in terms of resources than the other, the former may opt to foot the bill for one or two of the largest expenditures such as paying for the venue or the catering.

Nowadays, with many couples waiting longer to get married, after having worked for a number of years, they can afford to settle a significant part of the expenses themselves.

Honest and open communication very early on, is key to ensure that the whole experience has as little friction as possible. A frank discussion with representatives of both families and the couple about what each party would be willing and able to contribute will help all stakeholders get a good sense of the couple's hopes and expectations for the day. This can be a somewhat awkward conversation, so sensitivity is important.

Don't feel bad if as a parent you can't afford very much for the wedding and don't get railroaded into something you really can't afford. A wedding does not have to cost millions.

Keeping Numbers Down

The biggest factor influencing costs is the sheer number of guests attending. Ideally one should be able to invite just the nearest and dearest, but this is almost impossible to achieve particularly in societies where large extended families and associates are the norm. Being firm about the numbers can save you hundreds of thousands, even millions, but might make you rather unpopular.

The destination wedding is a growing trend and can be a great solution for the couple that craves a special day without all the pomp and circumstance. By escaping to a faraway location with closest friends and family, a couple can avoid the huge and often unmanageable crowd, which can be a great way to save money on your wedding.

Destination weddings also take away some of the major stress that comes with planning an elaborate affair. Many venues will plan the whole event for you with the honeymoon built in. You can invite as many or as few people as you want, and they should pay their own way if they want to vacation and celebrate with you. It is a difficult choice for those with large families that might not be able to travel, but if a couple is not looking to please every single family member and friend, it can be a good option.

Create a Wedding Gift List

Don't be embarrassed about creating, and sending out, a wedding gift list. Most of your guests - family, friends and colleagues, would probably like to buy you a present; but if you don't want to end up with six toasters, four kettles and three water filters, you might as well state or make a list of your wants and needs to save you having to buy them for your new home.

The easiest way to let people know what you want or need is to insert a gift list into your invitations. If your favorite stores do not have a bridal service, introduce the idea to them and create one with them; some local stores even manage the list for you and deliver your gifts after the wedding. They will be happy for the business.

Don't Jeopardise Your Retirement in the Process

It's nice to always put your children first, but you cannot afford to sacrifice your retirement income to fund their weddings. As far as possible, you must always be able to take care of your own needs. If you don't take care of your retirement savings, there is no guarantee that your children will be able or willing to take care of you. It might be advantageous to move in with your children in your later years for care and companionship, but not because you are broke.

Putting away money for a wedding is secondary to contributing to your pension and retirement savings, and maintaining an emergency fund and up to date insurance; make these goals your priority.

Start Early, Plan Ahead

The same way you should be following a savings regime to fund your child's education, it is a good idea to put one in place to fund family weddings. Once you have passed the education financial hurdle, make this the next priority so you aren't caught without funds for your child's most special day.

Invest according to your time horizon, and allocate assets accordingly. If the expected wedding is still nearly five years away, you might want to consider investing in a portfolio of stocks and bonds that have the potential for capital growth. An equity fund could be an ideal choice, as it offers liquidity, flexibility, diversification and professional management.

For a wedding that's just less than a year away, you cannot afford to risk stock market volatility, so you should invest in short-term money market instruments; fixed deposits, bank savings accounts, or a money market mutual fund would be appropriate.

Use a Wedding Planner

Beyond saving valuable time, there are benefits in using a wedding or event planner. Even where you are on a restricted budget, as most couples are, a wedding planner will help you set a realistic wedding budget based on how much you have available to spend. The best ones usually come with a wealth of knowledge garnered from vast experience relating to wedding etiquette, paying attention to the minutest detail and handling last-minute hitches. They have worked closely with professional suppliers and will be able to recommend the best people for your special day. They should have a good rapport with the best suppliers including venues, caterers, photographers, as well as with you, the client, and should be in a position to negotiate discounts on your behalf. In most cases, a wedding planner will save you time stress and money.

Till Debt Us do Part

Many couples, or their families, decide that they must go all out for their wedding, throwing caution to the wind and pulling out all the stops even where they can't really afford to pay for it. Some will then take out wedding loans. Starting out in marriage heavily in debt is the cause of great stress for any newly married couple. For the bride and groom, as far as possible, it is best to avoid borrowing to finance the wedding and parents should try to discourage it. Don't let the wedding ruin the marriage. Few things can set a marriage to a shaky start more than money palaver.

If however, due to time constraints or short-term cash-flow problems, borrowing makes more sense than selling assets intended to fund other goals. Have a clear plan in place to quickly pay off the loan.

Far too many couples are so caught up in the euphoria of the wedding that they don't stop to discuss important issues such as personal finance. Research shows that financial concerns are among the most common sources of tension in relationships and have some part in most divorces; yet most couples go into marriage without ever broaching this subject. It may not be romantic, but it is important. After the excitement of the wedding ceremonies and all the festivities, be well-prepared to face a financial future together.

W

Wills

"The possibilities for trouble when you leave no will are nearly endless. A hostile relative might be able to acquire a share of your estate, for example, or a relative who is already well fixed might take legal precedence over needier."
- Ted Miller -

Wills

Wills don't kill. The fear of death in many societies often prevents many of us from making plans for this most inevitable life event. Things may be going rather well, so why dwell on morbid thoughts such as your own death? Estate planning can be emotionally difficult to deal with and many people actually feel that they face imminent death if they focus on this subject. On the contrary, by considering your own mortality and getting your affairs in order, you give yourself peace of mind and cushion the impact of your death on your loved ones, thereby helping to reduce the amount of stress during what can be a very painful time.

There are several estate planning tools and techniques; these include wills, trusts, gifts, retirement pension plans and life insurance policies. Such tools should form a part of your financial plan and pass from the wealth accumulation stage through wealth preservation and finally through to the control of the disposition of your wealth.

Of the various strategies, a will is the most common and is one of the most important steps you can take to determine who inherits your property and personal assets. You have loved ones and people that you care deeply about such as your spouse, children, grandchildren, siblings, parents, a dear friend, or a trusted servant who may rely on you for financial support. What will happen to them if you were to pass on? It can be devastating for your loved ones if you haven't left a will and pass away "intestate," leaving intestacy laws to determine how your estate is handled, which may not be in accordance with your own wishes had you written a will.

Who Gets What?

Take an inventory of your significant assets such as investments, retirement savings, insurance policies, real estate, business interests and any other personal property such as vehicles, artwork, or jewelry. Assign a value to each asset. Once you have made the list of all your material possessions, make a short list of the people and institutions such as charities or your alma mater that you wish to leave your assets to in the event of your death. It is common in some countries for men to designate their brother as next of kin, but this can have serious implications for their widows and children. Ideally, a spouse and the children should take precedence over other beneficiaries.

In some communities, it is the birthright of the eldest son to automatically inherit all if a will has not been put in place. Whilst, historically, this was in place to protect the family assets and ensure that family members were supported, in reality the traditional heir may not be the ideal beneficiary to protect the family's interests. Be cautious about leaving significant sums of money directly to very young people. Some children are ill-equipped to handle sudden wealth and may squander it all in the twinkling of an eye.

Inheritance can be a complicated issue. The inconvenience and unpleasant situations that arise when heirs squabble over who gets what may certainly occur if there is no will. By planning ahead you also protect your estate from unintended recipients. Be absolutely clear about your intentions; this will help avert any potential conflicts after your demise.

Who Will Look After Your Children?

If you have minor children, spend some time deciding who will act as their guardian should they become orphaned. This should be clearly stipulated in your will and your chosen guardians should be informed of your wishes during your lifetime to determine whether he or she is suitable, willing or indeed able to take on such an important role and responsibility.

Update Your Will Periodically

Your financial situation is fluid, and the value of your assets will change from time to time. An estate plan should be reviewed at least once every two or three years and certainly when there is any significant change in your personal or family situation such as a birth, marriage, divorce, or death.

Should your marital status change or should there be a new birth or an adoption in the family, revisit your will or life insurance policies to ensure that any new beneficiaries are taken care of. Wills can be amended via a codicil. However, where there is to be a significant change it makes sense to draw up a new will, using the original one as a reference point.

Keep Your Will in a Safe, Readily Accessible Place

As with all your other important documents, such as title deeds and insurance policies, wills can be lost, stolen, damaged, or destroyed. It can be very awkward when such documents and other necessary information cannot be found. Original documents can be kept with a lawyer or banker and keep a copy for yourself for easy reference. Create a list of where the all-important information can be located and give the list to someone you trust.

Funeral Arrangements

If you have specific wishes concerning your funeral, discuss this informally with your family. Much that will happen is ritualistic or traditional and as such can be carefully planned in advance, from the funeral ceremony and service to the burial arrangements and any entertainment thereafter. This will give your family one less thing to think about at such a difficult time.

In some societies funerals can be such an elaborate long, drawn-out series of ceremonies that they force family members to dip into their savings or to go into huge debt, thus jeopardising their own financial future for a life past. A new home may be hastily built for the lying-in-state ceremony just to show off to the community.

If you have lived like royalty and wish to be buried like royalty, do plan ahead and set aside funds specifically for such an event so that loved ones are not further burdened in an already stressful situation. For many of us, the term estate planning conjures up images of the elderly or the wealthy; estate planning is a must for anyone who has accumulated even a modest amount of wealth and wants a say in how it is distributed once they are no longer alive. Careful estate planning can reduce most of the feeding frenzy and the amount of stress and strain that often occurs after a loved one passes on. No matter what your net-worth is — whether you are married, single, a single parent, divorced, widowed, young, or old — it is important to have a basic estate plan in place. Be sure to put your affairs in order now.

W

Windfalls

"Some people will be able to build on a financial windfall whilst others become overwhelmed and regretfully, may end up far worse off than before."
- A-Z Of Personal Finance -

Windfalls

Have you ever experienced the thrill of receiving money that you weren't expecting? Whilst you might never be lucky enough to win the lottery, chances are that at some point in your life you will receive a significant amount of money. A financial windfall presents you with unique opportunities as well as challenges as you are faced with a plethora of saving and spending options.

It is estimated that up to 70 percent of those who receive a financial windfall will lose it within just a few years. No matter how you receive the money, whether expected or as a complete surprise through a gift, a bonus, a retirement or severance package, an inheritance or the sale of a business, here are some tips to help you make the most of it.

Not all windfalls are received under happy circumstances. A financial windfall may come from serious injury, a divorce settlement, a lawsuit, or a death. Receiving an inheritance, can leave heirs feeling somewhat overwhelmed by the sudden change in their fortunes.

The first 3-6 months after receiving a financial windfall should be a time of adjustment. Before you make major decisions such as moving home, changing jobs, booking a dream holiday or buying a new car, deposit the money in a money market account for a period, whilst you review and redefine your goals, educate yourself about money matters and make plans.

You have an opportunity to pay off your debt or at least to reduce it particularly the most expensive credit card debt. Your decision should be determined by the interest rate you are paying on the debt as compared with the investment return you envisage.

Most people simply do not have the time or the expertise to manage their wealth, especially where large sums are involved. A financial advisor, an accountant, a stockbroker and a lawyer with estate planning experience are some of the professionals that can help you navigate the numerous tax, financial and legal issues that you must consider as you establish short, medium and long-term plans and put appropriate structures in place. A review of your estate plan may involve revising or updating your will or trust, setting up a foundation, or donating to charity. Try to build your own basic knowledge; this will put you better the position to preserve your wealth.

It is tempting to want to embark on a spending spree and to live lavishly. Indulge a little and spend some of the money on something you have always wanted but perhaps could not afford. Your advisers will help you to create an asset allocation plan for your money taking into account how much risk or volatility you are comfortable with. It pays to be conservative at least initially. To reduce risk build a diversified portfolio to include liquid money market deposits, stocks, bonds, mutual funds and real estate.

It is surprising how quickly news of a financial windfall spreads. It can be particularly challenging dealing with family, friends and business associates who will approach you about loans, business deals and "lucrative" investment opportunities. Keep an eye open for interesting business opportunities that you can invest in and consider them carefully, but do not feel under any pressure to part with your money too early.

Having money comes with responsibility and makes it possible for you to positively affect the life of others, which in turn gives your own life a sense of meaning and purpose. Investigate philanthropic initiatives that are well aligned with your personal values and beliefs, and determine how best to lend your support. When properly managed, a windfall can provide benefits that will continue beyond the lifetime of the initial recipient and can grow into a lasting financial legacy.

X

Exit Strategy

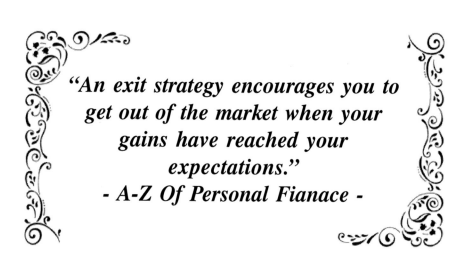

"An exit strategy encourages you to get out of the market when your gains have reached your expectations."

- A-Z Of Personal Fianace -

Exit Strategy

Emotions and Investing

Research has shown that people tend to remember the negative feelings of losing money far more acutely than the positive feelings associated with making profits. Whilst emotions can cloud judgment, you can minimise this influence on your investment decisions by having an exit strategy in place before you start investing and be committing yourself to sticking to it.

Developing an Exit Strategy

Consider some of these questions as you develop your exit strategy. For how long are you planning to invest? When should you get out? How much risk can you afford to take? How much of a loss are you prepared to take on a stock? Is it 10 percent, 20 percent or 30 percent? What's your target return from your investment? Whether it's an individual stock or a mutual fund, will you consider selling at least part of it after it's gone up say by 25 percent or 50 percent per cent? Revisit these questions, as your objectives and needs will certainly change over time.

Making an Exit

Isn't this scenario familiar? David paid $20 per share for ABC Plc shares. In a few months his shares were worth over $30 per share. Market noise suggested that ABC could hit $40 before long; David thought he might as well try to double his money before exiting. Then came a stock market crash. He kept holding on to the stock, hoping that it would soon recover. It didn't, and now ABC shares are selling for just $8 per share. With a clear exit strategy, David may have been able to dispassionately get out with perhaps only a 20% or 30% loss. What do you think you would you have done in that situation?

Buying stock is the easy part; but how do you know when to get out? Taking control of exits is easier said than done, as there is a delicate balance between selling too soon and holding on for too long. If you are a "buy and hold" investor, and the stock is rising, sometimes the hardest thing to do is to take profits as you don't want to exit prematurely; you can't help thinking about all the money you will miss out on if the price keeps going up. On the other hand, you don't want to see your "profit" disappear if the stock price reverses and begins a downward spiral.

Different tools have been developed for the purpose of protecting your profits from market volatility. Terms such as "take-profit" and "stop-loss" refer to the kind of exit being made. An exit strategy encourages you to get out of the market when your gains have reached your expectations. If you have already earned five years worth of gains according to your expectations, in just two to three years, why not sell and put the money in cash or other assets and wait for the market correction?

A stop order, will instruct your broker to sell if the stock price gets to a certain point, up or down. The sale directly controls locked-in profits or losses. This may be at a point at which you would lock in 90 percent of your profit; at least you would have kept most of your profit without having to put in a sell mandate in the middle of a market meltdown. This decision is made without any sentiment; the stop-order prompts you when it is time to quit, cut your losses and walk away.

Exit strategies determine the outcome of our investments. Remember you don't actually make any money until you sell a stock. Whilst these strategies will not guarantee you a profit or protect you from an absolute loss, they do reduce risk by helping you to make more reliable and realistic decisions devoid of emotion. Everyone will lose some money in the stock market at some point, but how much you lose is partially under your control and can be minimised. Unless you plan to hold a stock forever, whether your stocks are flourishing or failing, if you have no exit strategy, do consider putting one in place.

Y

Yield

"The rush for yield can easily lure inexperienced investors into areas that they are not familiar with. Be mindful of the fact that yield-seeking behaviour, when not carefully considered, can introduce substantial risks that derive from a lack of knowledge on the part of investors."
- A-Z Of Personal Finance -

Y

Yield

The Importance of Yield

Yield is an important part of any investment and is the investment income paid by many investments. The amount of money you make on an investment is directly related to how much you invest, and to the amount or yield you receive from it. Yield refers to investment income such as dividend income from stocks, coupon payments from bonds, interest payments from money-market funds and rental income from property that you earn each year as a percentage of what you spent on them. It is calculated by dividing the amount you receive annually by the amount you put into the investment.

Time to Adjust Expectations

For several years we became accustomed to earning double-digit returns on investments; it is time to adjust those expectations for what is more realistic. But that doesn't mean you can't keep looking for better yields. There are still some options when it comes to improving the earnings on your cash.

Some of these include high-yield current accounts, accounts that do not charge commission on turnover (COT). Bear in mind however that these special accounts do come with some restrictions; you might have a limited number of withdrawals in a month and are likely to have to maintain a minimum balance and there is likely to be a ceiling on the maximum balance that earns the higher rate.

Whilst it is worth shopping around for the best certificate of deposit rates and best savings accounts rates, always remember that the safety and security of your funds should be paramount. If this is indeed the most important consideration for you, then you might put your money in an account with a strong financial institution. If you are looking to increase your yield, and earning a bit more, you will have to move beyond the more traditional cash products and look towards higher-yielding instruments such as bonds and stocks.

Risk and Yield

With any investment you should always be conscious of your risk appetite, and an understanding of the concept of yield should always be considered in the context of the underlying risks before the investment decision is made. There is a trade off between liquidity, safety and yield; so one must carefully weigh these three factors as they relate to your unique circumstance. The most liquid investments with the least risk typically offer the lowest yields and hardly keep pace with inflation.

Be cautious in the world of stocks and bonds, as higher yields are accompanied by an exposure to a greater risk of loss. Generally, bonds offer a good stream of income, offer better returns than cash and a lower-risk profile than stocks; they offer a middle ground between cash and stocks in terms of risk and return. Low-rated bonds, which expose you to greater risk of default, must offer higher yields than stronger names in order to sell their securities.

Yield is a useful tool for comparing investment returns. Bernard earns $2,000 a year on an equity mutual fund in which he invested $10,000, and Gertrude earns the same amount in a money market account in which she deposited $20,000. Whilst their income is the same, the yield on their investments is different. The yield on Bernard's mutual fund is 20% and twice the yield on Gertrude's account, which is just 10%. Many investors are distracted by the "cash" being generated by their portfolios and don't realise that the yield may in fact be low.

Whilst yield helps you compare the performance of different investments, bear in mind that in comparing say a 2 percent stock yield to a 6 percent bond yield, there may be a stronger potential for the stock price to increase, providing a larger total return.

Dividends and Yield

A time when blue chip stocks, that is, stocks of well-established and financially sound companies are undervalued is an ideal time to select stocks that can provide decent returns and weather the market turbulence. It is useful to hold dividend-paying stocks in your portfolio not just as a substitute for cash investments, but as a complement to them. Some blue chip companies are somewhat reluctant to reduce or rescind dividend payments even in difficult times. If you hold the stock of solid, established companies that can comfortably manage their dividend payouts, you are likely to have a fairly predictable source of income, which can provide a cushion in a volatile market. Indeed, dividend cheques have replaced many a retirees' monthly salary cheques as a regular source of income that can make up for some of the low yields being paid on cash.

Remember that a high-yielding investment does not necessarily indicate a sound investment. Dividends are not necessarily only paid by strong, well-established companies with strong earnings. Seek out companies that have a long history of sustaining and increasing their dividend payments rather than those struggling to pay dividends when they don't really have the cash or business basis to support this.

When you invest in a bear market, as stock prices fall, dividend yields improve significantly. Yet this tends to be the time when most of us hesitate to put our money into the stock market due to fear and pessimism. For example, if a company's share price is $25 and it pays a dividend of 50 cents per share, the yield is 2 percent. If the company is still committing to paying 50 cents per share as the share price rises or falls, the yield will change. So, say the price increased to $35, the yield would fall to 1.4 percent. If on the other hand the price fell to $20, the yield would rise to 2.5 percent.

The rush for yield can easily lure inexperienced investors into areas that they are not familiar with. Be mindful of the fact that yield-seeking behaviour, when not carefully considered, can introduce substantial risks that derive from a lack of knowledge on the part of investors. There is a tendency for investors to be lured into investments based on past performance. Always keep in view the premise that past performance is not an indicator of and does not predict future performance.

Z

Zero-Based Budget

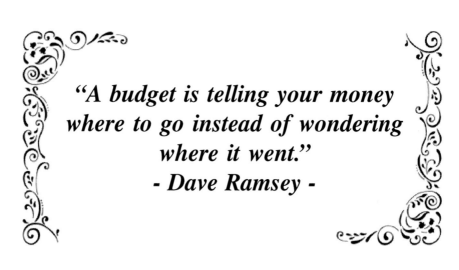

"A budget is telling your money where to go instead of wondering where it went."
- Dave Ramsey -

Zero-Based Budget

To many people the word "budgeting" smacks of being an unpleasant, tedious activity. Think of a budget, rather as a tool to give you a clear financial spending plan that will help you to manage your money.

Are you spending more than you earn? Are your finances out of control? We all have income, and we all have expenses, and often we do not know where all the money goes. A budget will help you take control of your money by providing you with a concrete, organised breakdown of how much money you have coming in, and how much of it you are spending; this will help you keep track of where your money comes from and where it goes. Here are some points to note when preparing a monthly personal budget:

Calculate Your Income

We all tend to have a good idea of the main sources of our income; our monthly salaries, and any additional income such as rental or dividend income, commissions and bonuses that we might earn. Calculate exactly how much income you have coming in.

Track Your Expenses

It is keeping track of expenses that most people tend to struggle with. It is easy to monitor the regular expenses such as rent, insurance and utility bills, but it is the cash and daily "hidden" expenses that you don't even remember spending that are more difficult to track.

Planning and monitoring your budget will help you to identify those expenses that you often cannot account for. Chart all your daily spending for a month or two. Record every expense, from buying your daily newspaper, to picking up an appliance at the mall, to eating out, or filling your car tank; this is the only way you can get a true picture of what you are actually doing with your money and have a better chance of cutting back on excesses and adjusting your spending patterns if need be. When you actually see the breakdown of your expenses, you will be surprised to find how quickly things add up.

Are You Living within Your Means?

Once you have totaled up your monthly income and your monthly expenses, subtract the expenses from the income and see what is left. If there is nothing left or worse still, if your expenses far exceed your income, you will need to aggressively trim your expenses and try to live within your means so that you can begin to work towards accomplishing your goals.

Stick to it

The hardest part of budgeting is sticking to the budget; many people tell me that whilst they found setting up their budget easy, when it came to living within it, they failed. Remember, you are the only one that can maintain a budget, so it should be tailored to your needs, your values and your priorities. Start by setting specific goals for yourself such as making a down payment on a property, or taking a family holiday. Focusing on set, achievable goals will give you something to work towards and help you stay within your budget.

Keep it Simple

In preparing a budget it is important to keep things simple and straightforward. If your budget is too complicated you will quickly abandon it. There are several budgeting tools ranging from simple worksheets that can be downloaded free of charge from the Internet and customised with spending categories appropriate to your lifestyle, to more sophisticated personal finance software such as Quicken or Microsoft Money. The built-in budget making tools can create your budget for you. The key is to find the right tool that works for you.

A zero-based budget helps you allocate all your expenses, by placing all your income sources into categories; the goal is to account for every single dollar that you receive so that it tallies with your expenses and is already assigned to a particular need.

Take for example, your monthly income is $2,000, ideally anything that you spend or save, give or invest should equal exactly $2,000. Most of us do not know where our money goes and this is a fundamental issue if you are on a path to wealth creation and staying on course with your budget. You must be able to account for everything.

As you save and invest towards future purchases such as car or a house, entertainment, vacations, which may vary from month to month, add an "unexpected events category" to take care of emergencies and variables. When this Zero-Based Budget is properly created, everything you spend can be accounted for and money is set aside regularly to cover each expense as it is required.

Budgeting is one of the most effective tools in your quest for financial success as it helps you to you prioritise your spending and manage your money, irrespective of how much or how little you have. The earlier you start, the better; for young people who start to keep a budget, this sense of financial clarity will become a habit that will serve them well throughout their lives. Whatever your goals are, paying off your debt, buying a house, or educating your children, your budget forms the foundation of your financial plan and will help you down the road to long-term financial security.

ABOUT THE AUTHOR

Nimi Akinkugbe is the founder and Chief Executive Officer of Bestman Games Ltd, a leading games company and the African distributor of customised editions of Hasbro's Monopoly game. The City of Lagos Edition of Monopoly, the first African city edition of Monopoly, was launched in December 2012.

She enjoyed a successful banking career spanning 23 years, first at Stanbic IBTC Bank Plc where she rose to the position of General Manager and Head, Private Banking and Director of Stanbic IBTC Asset Management Limited, and subsequently at Barclays Bank Plc where she was Regional Director (West Africa) for the Wealth & Investment Management Division and Chief Country Officer for Nigeria.

Through the Monopoly board game, speaking engagements, television and radio appearances and other media, Nimi seeks to promote financial literacy as a tool for economic empowerment. She regularly contributes articles to a host of publications including *Genevieve* Magazine, a leading women's lifestyle magazine, *The Punch* Newspapers, *BusinessDay* and *Forbes Africa*. Her articles are also featured on websites and blogs including Bella Naija, Lagos Mums, Eden Lifestyle and *The Edition*, a Kenyan Publication. Through these fora she is able to create a greater awareness and understanding of personal finance and wealth management issues.

Nimi has a Bachelors Degree from The London School of Economics (LSE) and an MBA from IESE, International Graduate School of Management. She also formalised her interest in music by obtaining a Piano Teaching Diploma, ARCM (Pianoforte) from The Royal College of Music, London.

She is a member of the Board of Trustees of the Ajumogobia Science Foundation, a member of the Executive Council of Women in Management, Business & Public Service (WIMBIZ), a member of the Selection Committee of the Tony Elumelu Entrepreneurship Programme and a member of the Artistes Committee of the Musical Society of Nigeria (MUSON). She is on the board of The Play Pen (Child Development Centre), The Daisy Management Centre, House of Tara and Financial Derivatives Company Ltd.

She is a keen gardener and enjoys writing, boating, playing the piano and traveling. She is married with 3 children.

Index

Lightning Source UK Ltd.
Milton Keynes UK
UKOW02f1534291116
288799UK00001B/86/P